ALL IN

ALL IN

Expanding Access through
Nationally Competitive Awards

THE NATIONAL ASSOCIATION OF
FELLOWSHIPS ADVISORS

Edited by Suzanne McCray

THE UNIVERSITY OF ARKANSAS PRESS
FAYETTEVILLE
2013

Copyright © 2013 by The University of Arkansas Press

ISBN-10: 1-55728-640-X
ISBN-13: 978-1-55728-640-6
e-ISBN: 978-1-61075-528-3

17   16   15   14   13   5   4   3   2   1

Designer: Ellen Beeler
Cover design and photographs: Crystal McBrayer

∞ The paper used in this publication meets the minimum requirements of the American National Standard for Permanence of Paper for Printed Library Materials Z39.48-1984.

Cataloging-in-Publication Data on file at the Library of Congress.

Contents

Foreword

Two hundred fifty—that is the number of guest rooms we told Chicago's Drake Hotel we would need each night during Broadening Opportunities, Encouraging Diversity, the July 2011 sixth biennial National Association of Fellowships Advisors (NAFA) national conference. In the year leading up to the conference, the planners at times worried whether we had over-committed and would be able to fulfill our contract with the Drake. We particularly worried that the economy and university budget constraints would keep people from attending. After all, these are lean times in academia, and perhaps that year would be the one NAFA members tell us that though they really, really wanted to attend, darn it, they just couldn't find the money.

Our worrying was for naught. We watched our room count quickly tick up and pass the 250 mark six weeks before the conference started. Before we knew it, we were contracting for more rooms at the Drake, asking if nearby hotels could handle our overflow, and sending ever-more-harried reminders to the NAFA Listserv that if members had not booked a room yet, they might want to take care of that right now.

We ended up with 336 registered conference goers, a one-third increase from our Seattle conference just two years prior. That level of growth would be remarkable for any organization, let alone for one during poor economic times. So what is going on here? My instincts say that our growth is primarily fueled by the remarkable attitude and good nature of our members. NAFA conferences just feel different. In general, I do not consider myself to be a conference guy. I do not like being away from my family, on someone else's schedule, paying money for events that are sometimes of dubious quality. But ever since I attended my first NAFA event, I have been hooked. NAFAns are generous, almost to a fault. We share information and best practices even though we are all engaged in zero-sum competitions. It would be easy for all of us to take our ball and go home, but we choose to share, to collaborate, to celebrate student victories even when they are not ours. Of special note are our foundation and overseas partners, who patiently answer all of our questions, down to the most minute, obsessive details (Should that be stapled or paper-clipped? is not too fine a question for a NAFAn).

I also think that people attend and loyally return to NAFA events because they find a plethora of high-quality advice. The nature of our membership means that our speakers tend to be well-educated people who are deeply thoughtful about their work and how to present it to others. The 2011 conference also included two exceptional people who helped us focus on our conference theme. John Brown Jr., the associate director of the White House Initiative on Historically Black Colleges, spoke about the intersection of higher education, diversity, and scholarship advising. During our closing banquet, keynote speaker Debbie Bial, founder of the Posse Foundation and recipient of a MacArthur "Genius Grant," gave a charged and provocative speech questioning our very concept of *merit* and how we measure it in our society. These speeches—along with the thirty-nine concurrent sessions, the thirteen foundation presentations, the New Advisor's workshop, the half-day symposium on higher educa-tion in Ireland, the breakfast and dessert roundtable discussions, and our regular guided conversation about ethics in scholarship advising—made for a busy (some might say exhausting), rewarding, and completely full conference schedule.

With all of that activity, not to mention our summer study travels and off-year summer workshops, it would be easy for NAFA to rest on its laurels or just keep the same formula. But NAFAns, like the students we advise, are full of ideas and work hard to realize them. Thanks to NAFA's past presidents Paula Warrick and Jane Morris, we are in the middle of enacting a five-year strategic plan to make the organization even more meaningful and important to its members. In the coming years, we can look forward to an improved website, further outreach to institutions that serve traditionally underrepresented constituencies, and an annual survey of the profession. We are also encouraging NAFAns to connect to other scholarship advisors in their region, offering funds for smaller gatherings that might attract new institutions to join us, or to offer postconference information and highlights to schools that could not join us.

As we do so, we have the additional challenge of staying true to our core mission and to NAFA's value of placing process over outcomes. Another reason for our constant growth is that universities increasingly are seeing the value of having their students receive national scholarships and so are investing more resources in this area. That is, in general, a positive development for our field, but only when tempered with both realistic views of the perceived power we have as advisors to create scholars and a focus on student development instead of counting winners. By redefining *winning* as "student development," "goal setting," and "self-awareness," we can assure positive outcomes for all of our applicants, whether or not they receive an award. NAFA has played and must continue to play an important and leading role in shaping higher education's conversation on this topic. The essays included in this volume are a part of that conversation.

This is an exciting time for NAFA, and it is hard to believe that we are only a twelve-year-old all-volunteer organization. Thanks to the work of many members, board members, officers, and foundation representatives, we are poised to continue to improve and grow into the future, seeking to fulfill our mission "to guide advisors in promoting the full potential of fellowship candidates through the application process, and to foster the continued growth and professionalization of fellowship advising in higher education." I look forward to continuing on that journey with all of you.

Doug Cutchins
NAFA President, 2011–13

Acknowledgments

The National Association of Fellowships Advisors (NAFA) held its sixth biennial conference in Chicago in July 2011. Many of the essays included in this volume grew out of the discussions held there. The conference could not have taken place without the hard work of a significant number of people. Jane Morris (Villanova University), who was president of NAFA at the time of the conference, deserves special recognition for her significant contribution to NAFA both during the conference and throughout its history. Doug Cutchins (Grinnell College) was the vice president when the conference occurred and assumed the role of president at the conference's end. The vice president is the main organizer of the event, which includes inviting speakers, calling for papers, negotiating with hotels, coordinating panels, and a long list of other responsibilities. He had significant help from experienced NAFA conference organizer Beth Powers (University of Illinois–Chicago), who chaired the Chicago Working Group. NAFA treasurer John Richardson (University of Louisville) and Paula Goldsmid (Pomona College), who was NAFA secretary, were also instrumental in making the event happen. Other conference planners and special contributors include Alex Trayford (Wheaton College), Alicia Hayes (University of California–Berkeley), Amanda Harrison (University of Illinois–Chicago), Amanda Norton (University of Chicago), Babs Wise (Duke University), Carol Madison Graham (Marshall Aid Commemoration Commission), Cindy Schaarschmidt (Drexel University), Dana Kuchem (The Ohio State University), David Schug (University of Illinois), Denise DellaRosa (University of Notre Dame), Elizabeth Lewis Pardoe (Northwestern University), Eugene Alpert (The Washington Center), Graciela Guzman (Grinnell College), Hilarion Marinez (Florida International University), Jeff Wing (Virginia Commonwealth College), Jennifer Keating-Miller (Carnegie Mellon University), Jill Deans (University of Connecticut), John Pearson

(Stanford University), Julia Goldberg (Lafayette College), Karna Walters (University of Arizona), Kathleen Harris (Loyola Marymount University), Kimberly Germain (New York University), Kristin Osiecki (University of Illinois–Chicago), Kyle Mox (Texas A&M University), Laure Pengelly Drake (University of Montana), Lisa Knepshield (University of Illinois–Chicago), Liz Veatch (NAFA communications director), Lowell Frye (Hampden-Sydney College), Luke Green (Seattle University), Margaret Tongue (Union College), Mary Cookie Sunkle (Denison University), Mary Denyer (Marshall Aid Commemoration Commission), Mona Pitre-Collins (University of Washington), Monique Bourque (Willamette University), Narjis Abdul-Majid (University of Louisville), Nicole Gelfert (University of Central Florida), Paula Warrick (American University), Roberta Jordan (University of Notre Dame), Robin Chang (University of Washington), Sigmund Burdin (University of Illinois at Chicago), Steve Wright (Syracuse University), Susan Sharp (NSEP/Boren), Tim Dolan (Westminster College), Tony Cashman (College of the Holy Cross), Tony Claudino (Fulbright Grants), and all those who presented at the conference.

The active participation of foundations during national and regional conferences is critical to the continued success of NAFA in providing advisors with accurate and appropriate information to share with their students. The foundation representatives who were particularly unstinting in their contribution to the Chicago conference include Amra Dusic (DAAD Scholarships International), Carol Madison Graham (Marshall Aid Commemoration Commission), Cathy Makunga (Hispanic Scholarship Fund), Doris Carver (National Science Foundation Graduate Research Fellowships Program), Elliot Gerson (The Rhodes Scholarship), James Smith (Gates Cambridge Scholarships), Jane Curlin (Morris K. Udall and Stewart L. Udall Scholarship Foundation Scholarships), Jennifer Campbell (Benjamin A. Gilman International Scholarship Program), Jose Zambrana (EPA Fellowships), Laurie Hardy (Thomas R. Pickering Foreign Affairs Fellowship Program), Malaika Serrano (Critical Language Scholarship Program), Mary Denyer (Marshall Aid Commemoration Commission), Meredith Burlew (Rotary Scholarships), Mike Lenardo (NIH Oxford Cambridge Scholar Program), Nicole Sisco (Robert Bosch Foundation Fellowship Program), Patricia Scroggs, (Charles B. Rangel International Affairs Program), Peggy Petrochenkov

(Ford Foundation Fellowship Program), Renee Reiling (Rotary Scholarships), Sandy Junge (Barry Goldwater Scholarship), Stan Heginbotham (Paul and Daisy Soros Fellowships for New Americans), Susan Sharp (Boren Awards for International Study), Tara Yglesias (Harry S. Truman Scholarship Foundation), Tom Parkinson (The Beinecke Scholarship), Tonly Claudino (Fulbright U.S. Student Program), and Trina Vargo (George Mitchell Scholarship Program). Keynote speakers John Brown Jr. (Office of the White House Initiative on Historically Black Colleges and Universities) and Deborah Bial (founder and president of the Posse Foundation) set the tone of the conference, which focused on broadening opportunities and encouraging diversity.

For this volume of essays, special thanks go to the NAFA Publications Board, especially cochairs Nicole Gelfert (University of Central Florida) and Tara Yglesias (Harry S. Truman Scholarship Foundation). Annie Livingston (chief of staff to the cochair of the Bill and Melinda Gates Foundation) was also very helpful in providing permission to include the address William Gates Sr. gave at the 2009 conference.

Thanks go, as well, to the staff of Enrollment Services at the University of Arkansas and to the Office of Nationally Competitive Awards, in particular. Jason Blankenship (associate director) and Jack Ayres (graduate assistant) provided excellent proofreading help, and Crystal McBrayer (the director of communication for Enrollment Services) designed the cover. The ongoing support of Chancellor G. David Gearhart, Provost Sharon Gaber, and Dean Tom Smith has helped make this publication possible, as have the efforts of the University of Arkansas Press: Larry Malley, director; Brian King, director of editing, design, and production; and Julie Watkins, editor.

ALL IN

Introduction

This collection of essays grew out of the NAFA conference Broadening Opportunities, Encouraging Diversity held in Chicago in 2011. Some of the essays are the direct result of presentations given at the conference; others developed later. All concern expanding opportunities for a greater number of talented students across the country and deepening the value of the scholarship experience for all who apply. The title of this volume, *All In: Expanding Access through Nationally Competitive Awards,* reflects the overall attitude of advisors and foundation representatives about their scholarship and fellowship efforts. As many of the essays make clear, advising and supporting applicants for nationally and internationally competitive awards are not for the faint hearted and require an ability both to cope with a variety of challenges and to keep the real purposes of the work in mind.

Even as our colleges and universities aspire to increase the number and the diversity of student applicants, many foundations are making hard choices as they face shrinking resources and the complex challenges of a tough economy. Some have cut costs by reducing the number of interviews, asking students or institutions to pay travel, cutting awards to students who receive honorable mentions, and so on. The Mitchell, in particular, faced an uncertain future, mobilizing a national outcry that saved it in 2012. All of these actions have been done in an effort to sustain as many scholarships as possible.

And the number of talented students applying for these limited opportunities has grown, so broadening opportunities and expanding access through nationally competitive awards must mean something beyond winning a scholarship. The essays in this volume address what expanding access through nationally competitive awards means to students, advisors, institutions, and foundations.

"Democratizing the World of Scholarships," the first essay in this volume, is a keynote address given by William Gates, Sr. at a NAFA conference in Seattle in 2009. It has not appeared in a previous NAFA publication and is included here because it so perfectly sets the tone for a work about increasing access and expanding opportunity. Gates makes clear that encouraging students to believe in themselves, to fully explore their potential, and to act boldly and confidently is as important as their winning scholarships. Advisors are charged with broadening their sense of what it means to be talented, encouraging widely, and actively engaging with students who may not fit the traditional model of a successful candidate.

The charge from Gates is similar to one made in "Strengthening Nationally Competitive Scholarships: Thoughts from an International Conference in Bellagio," in *Beyond Winning: National Scholarship Competitions and the Student Experience* (Fayetteville: University of Arkansas, 2005): "We believe that talent is broadly, even randomly, distributed, but only selectively developed" (67). By encouraging a particular student to apply for an award, an advisor makes clear an admiration for and a confidence in that student. As Gates advises, encouraging a student who otherwise might not have anything to do with a scholarship could open other doors for her. As the Bellagio report continues, it surely is "worthwhile to enlarge the pool even at the expense of having more disappointed people—those worthy, but not chosen" (67). Having a student apply for a nationally competitive award can change the way a student sees herself and the way a faculty member views her, as well. This can affect letters of recommendation, graduate school considerations, and long-range goals.

The three essays that follow are from foundations. Truman Foundation executive secretary Andrew Rich focuses on the Truman's summer program for its scholars. The program is designed to expand opportunities beyond funding for graduate school and to help scholars assess and strengthen long-term commitments to public service. Rich emphasizes that for many students such programming can be even more important than scholarship dollars.

In chapter 3, Deputy Executive Secretary Tara Yglesias addresses the Truman interview. She provides practical advice about what makes up an interview and what does not. She dispels myths, outlines expectations, and encourages calm. She also stresses that being interviewed for a Truman Scholarship is a valuable experience in itself. Finalists learn from the interviewers and from each other. They build friendships and connect with those with shared values (if not similar ideas).

In chapter 4, John Lanning and Goldwater Scholarship president Frank Gilmore also extend practical advice for anyone applying for or advising someone who is applying for the Goldwater. As with the Truman, faculty representatives can nominate up to four students to compete for the scholarship. Most research institutions have many more qualified applicants than they can accommodate. Therefore, students should outline past research, determine the most appropriate graduate programs for their interests, and succinctly write about a completed project or one that is in progress. The value of the scholarship program extends far beyond the 1,200 who are nominated and the 300 who win. The program itself, like so many others in the sciences (DOE, DOD, NSF GRFP, NDSEG, etc.), not only rewards students but also encourages them to engage in undergraduate research as early and as meaningfully as possible and, by doing so, to increase their preparation and competitiveness for postgraduate study.

Chapter 5, Richard Montauk's essay on advising students who are applying for law school, cautions advisors to make certain that law school really is the right fit. Montauk stresses that students' decision-making process for law school is much like deciding if a particular scholarship will allow them to accomplish long-term goals. His advice is pragmatic and will be helpful to anyone preparing to apply to competitive law schools.

The remaining seven chapters focus on various aspects of scholarship advising: increasing diversity, managing workloads, building partnerships with administration, controlling expectations, and continuing to develop professionally. In chapter 6, Carol Madison Graham addresses diversity, examining why the statistics on African Americans studying abroad is low. She encourages advisors to actively recruit with an understanding of historical and social factors that might lead to a reluctance to participate. Graham provides advice based on her extensive experience as the executive director of the UK Fulbright Commission and from her personal experiences as a minority abroad. According to the Institute on International Education, the number of African Americans who study abroad is increasing, from 3.5 percent in 2005–6 to 4.8 percent in 2010–11 (still low but at least on the rise). Graham's practical tips on increasing diverse participation in study abroad programs can help any campus expand its recruitment efforts and continue to increase these numbers.

"Honoring the Code" addresses the ethics of advising, a much-discussed topic in NAFA. The essay's origin is a talk given at a plenary session at the 2011 Chicago conference, which was followed by a workshop that examined various scenarios and possible ethical responses. The discussion was lively, and the ethical situations examined clearly were complex enough to solicit active disagreement. This essay provides a background of problematic student behavior in colleges and universities and outlines suggestions for safeguarding the process from student, advisor, faculty, and institution view points. The essay also places advising in a larger educational framework that provides students with learning experiences beyond the individual application.

The following essay "Recalculating: A Sojourn Down Scholarship Road to the Deep Heart's Core" begins with Elizabeth Vardaman recounting her disappointment when a student she has come to admire receives the news that he has not been selected to receive a scholarship. But the essay is much more than a personal memoir that recounts the misery all advisors know. Like the essay on ethics, this piece makes a convincing case that the process provides a venue for intellectual engagement for both the student and the advisor: "They give me hope for the future—all of them making a difference somewhere, somehow—fighting injustice, creating beauty, seeking truth, mending lives, and working hard to bring light to dark places. And they have made me better than I meant to be." Expanding access does not simply refer to the world of students.

The next two chapters focus on the stresses of scholarship advising. "Coping with Common Challenges: Strategies for Success in Fellowship Advising" provides six scenarios that advisors might face while working with selection committees, faculty members, and supervisors. After each scenario, authors Dana Kuchem, Beth Powers, and Susan Whitbourne suggest various ways for handling these situations. "Balancing Scholarship and Scholarship Advising" also addresses the work lives of advisors, outlining ways to combine productive advising with active involvement in professional development and even scholarship. These two chapters also stress that advising is part of the teaching mission of colleges and universities and should be approached as such by the advisors and by those who supervise them.

Beth Powers's essay on the history and purpose of NAFA, stresses that it is an organization dedicated to expanding access in a variety of ways. This expansion includes broadly sharing accurate information with talented students across the country, many of whom might not otherwise have a solid understanding about what is expected, and assisting previously underrepresented institutions with building professional advising offices with staff trained to deliver accurate information about the process as it relates to specific scholarships. The foundations are a critical part of this training, and without their active participation in meetings, workshops, and study tours, such educational outreach and expansion of access would not be possible. NAFA has worked hard to include smaller schools, two-year colleges, historically black colleges and universities, and liberal arts colleges. And of course, sustaining and improving access for students means regular training for all advisors. Making clear to advisors and, subsequently, to students how the process works is access in itself. Transparency opens doors.

The final essay by former NAFA president Jane Morris, provides a personal example that sums up what a student who learns of a good opportunity can make of it. She outlines a way to move beyond traditional ways of identifying students so that more students can be encouraged to consider special opportunities and view themselves as part of the worthy many who may indeed become one of the lucky few. Morris ties her experiences back to William Gates Sr.'s charge that "perhaps most important of all you encourage students to believe in themselves. . . . Part of your task is to give them the confidence to be bold when thinking about what's in store for them." Advisors encourage students to act boldly, to take risks for the good that may be in store for them and for the good they have the potential to bring to others. As the Bellagio report reminds us, "Missing their potential contribution deprives not only them, but also us." And so advisors, institutions, and foundations are all in, working together to realize the mission of promoting "the full potential of fellowship candidates through the application process," whether they win a scholarship or not.

Suzanne McCray
University of Arkansas

1

Democratizing the World of Scholarships

WILLIAMS GATES SR.

William Gates Sr., *appointed in 1997 by then-governor Gary Locke, was a regent at the University of Washington until September 2012. He is cochair of the Bill & Melinda Gates Foundation and a former trustee for the Gates Cambridge Trust. He has brought to these roles a distinguished career in law and many years of work and public service in local, national, and international communities. Having received his baccalaureate and law degrees from the University of Washington, Gates has continued to give back to the University of Washington, generously contributing to the law school, intercollegiate athletics, and diversity initiatives, among other areas. He was chair of the foundation board from 2001 to 2006, and his leadership of Campaign UW: Creating Futures has helped ensure the future strength of the institution. He delivered the following address as regent of the University of Washington at a conference of the National Association of Fellowships Advisors held in Seattle on July 18, 2009.*

It is humbling to be here. Of course, I am impressed by the caliber of the people in this room. It is wonderful that you have formed this association to think collaboratively about your work. But what is really striking is the caliber of people you are responsible for sending out into the world. The fellowships that the foundations represented here offer—and that the advisors here help students earn—open doors for these incredible people.

I first came to know the world of fellowships when my son and his wife established the Gates Cambridge Scholarship. They asked me to serve as a trustee, and I have been doing that for ten years. One of the best parts of my job is traveling to Cambridge every spring to meet with the scholars and learn a little bit more about their research interests and their day-to-day lives. I am continually blown away by the quality of young people I meet there—both their intellectual quality and their extraordinary expectations.

I know full well that I would experience the same exhilaration visiting any cohort of the scholars chosen in your process. On a recent trip I met a young scholar from Australia, Dr. Alice Chang. Dr. Chang is an ophthalmologist. She used to spend her time flying to remote places to treat aboriginal people who had no other access to an eye doctor. She literally landed in the bush and performed eye surgery on the spot.

But that was not enough for Dr. Chang. While she was caring for her patients, she noticed how many untreated health problems they had. In particular, she realized that some of them suffered from psychological illnesses that undermined their quality of life. So she took it upon herself to do something. She applied for a Gates Cambridge Scholarship. Now, she is getting a degree in psychology so she can go back to Australia and serve her patients twice as effectively. What I find so inspiring about Dr. Chang is not just her boundless ambition and talent but the fact that it is pointed in the direction of addressing inequity.

Your work should include an element of this same ambition. Whether you are affiliated with a college or with a foundation, I know you are focused on making sure everyone has equal access to the fellowship process. That is one of the reasons you came here for this meeting, to devise the best strategies for democratizing the world of fellowships. There are Dr. Changs everywhere, and you are committed to finding them.

When it comes to the hard work of democratizing, you are both a scout and a coach. You find the young people with the most talent, and then you nurture that talent. Perhaps most important of all, you encourage students to believe in themselves. And you also encourage professors to believe in their students.

It is true at all levels there are young people whose potential is much greater than they think it is. Many don't think about fellowship opportunities at all, because they simply aren't encouraged to see their futures in that way. Others assume they are not cut out for the top fellowships. Part of your task is to give them the confidence to be bold when thinking about what is in store for them—and to help their professors be just as bold.

I just witnessed a great example of encouragement when I visited LaGuardia Community College in Queens, New York. LaGuardia is a temple to our democratic ideals. It is a place where everybody can get in—and if they work hard, they can find rewarding work and a better future. In fact, LaGuardia is the most diverse postsecondary institution in the world. It has students from more countries than any of its counterparts.

Again, my favorite part of the visit was the hour or so I spent talking with the students. I met one young man in particular who had only recently emigrated from Niger. One of his professors suggested he run for student government. He told me that after that conversation, his whole mind-set changed. He told me, and I am quoting here, "I feel that I can do that, and I am going to try it."

Not to say he was not ambitious; he emigrated across an ocean and is supporting himself through college, which is quite a feat in itself. Even so, it took something extra, the confidence his professor showed in him, the encouragement, to help him believe in his own potential.

You have dedicated your careers to being encouragers. I would like to ask you today to broaden your concept of encouragement. Because it is not just students who need encouragement, it's everybody on every college campus. The prevailing idea seems to be that there are a few students who are fellowship material—and a few schools that produce them—and there are the rest of the students, and everybody knows who belongs in each group. That is an elitist viewpoint whose time is past. Talent does not manifest itself in just one way. Many young people who are not considered "elites" are in fact elite from an intellectual perspective. So another way you can be an encourager is by encouraging those who stuck with the old notion of what talent looks like or where talent comes from to change their minds.

I urge you to help professors commit themselves to the same democratizing ideals that have run through this conference. Hammer that point home with them. If they start thinking about connecting more young people to the great opportunities a college campus offers, then you will have more great applicants. In the end, we will all be better off for it. Because as more and more individuals reach their full potential, we as a society inch ever closer to reaching our full potential.

I will not soon forget the recommendation letter I read for one of the 2006 Gates Cambridge Scholars, a young lady named Molly Crockett. The letter was from her very eminent professor at UCLA, and what stood out most was his story of his first memory of Molly. When she was just about to graduate high school, she found his name and called him up to ask whether UCLA was the best school to attend if she wanted to get into a top graduate program in cognitive neuroscience. He was impressed by her motivation and intellect, not to mention by the courage it takes for a seventeen-year-old to cold-call a professor.

He said that yes, UCLA can get you where you want to go, but only if you get involved with research from the beginning. And he offered her a position in his lab working with graduate students. He encouraged her to set her sights high.

Three years later, Molly was presenting results from a paper she had coauthored to the Cognitive Neuroscience Society, something usually reserved for graduate students. Now, she is at Cambridge, getting her doctorate and exploring how to use her education to advocate for better public health policies. The professor who wrote the recommendation said it very clearly: Molly was the best student he had ever seen. What I would add is that Molly had, in addition to fine personal attributes, a professor who was an encourager.

That is the kind of talent you are responsible for. And that talent is not particular to students like Molly Crockett, not particular to students from one country, one set of universities—or even one scholarship program. If you can succeed in the task of making both students and their professors believe that, then you will have made an important contribution to the establishment of equity in this great work you are about.

Thank you and good luck.

2

Broadening Horizons and Building Community
The Truman Foundation's Summer Institute

ANDREW RICH

Andrew Rich became executive secretary of the Harry S. Truman Scholarship Foundation in October 2011. He directs the independent federal agency that provides merit-based Truman Scholarships to college students who plan to attend graduate school in preparation for careers in public service. Before joining the Truman Foundation, Rich was president and CEO of the Roosevelt Institute, a nonprofit organization devoted to carrying forward the legacy and values of Franklin and Eleanor Roosevelt. Rich is the author of Think Tanks, Public Policy, and the Politics of Expertise *(2004), as well as a number of wide-ranging articles on the role of experts and ideas in the American policy process. He was chair of the Political Science Department at the City College of New York before joining the Roosevelt Institute. From 1999 to 2003, he taught political science at Wake Forest University. He received his bachelor's from the University of Richmond and his PhD in political science from Yale University. He was a 1991 Truman Scholar from Delaware.*

When the first class of Truman Scholars was selected in 1977, the freshly minted scholars—all college sophomores—were flown to Independence, Missouri, for a weekend ceremony to be recognized among their peers and sent off with $20,000 in scholarship support. The money *was* the award. Back then, scholars received support for their last two years of college and the first portion of a graduate program, and they met each other only that one time. From there, we sent them off to finish their educations with independence from one another and from the Truman Scholarship Foundation.

Times have changed, and so has the Truman Scholar experience. During the past thirty-five years, the number and types of graduate programs relevant to public service have multiplied, as have the challenges facing leaders in public service. In response the mandate of the Truman Foundation has evolved such that we not only provide financial support to an outstanding collection of individual change agents but also seek to build community among them through programming. Community building among Truman Scholars strengthens their knowledge of the diverse paths to public service leadership; it deepens their commitment to lead and work in collaboration with others; and it forms bonds of lasting friendship that inevitably provide support during challenging times, both personal and professional.

Summer Institute

The Truman Foundation's Summer Institute is central to these efforts. In the summer that occurs a year following their selection (and, therefore, typically just after they finish college), the scholars spend nine weeks in Washington, DC, participating in paid internships in the public or nonprofit sectors and in a wide variety of seminars and workshops focused on professional and personal development. Scholars spend the summer living together in residence halls centrally located in downtown Washington, and foundation staff members focus on providing the group with mentoring and fellowship opportunities.

Truman Scholars arrive in Washington, DC, for Summer Institute around Memorial Day, and they spend their first week participating in workshops that acquaint them with the city, with leaders from all corners of public service, and with some of the challenges they can expect to face during the course of the summer. In 2011, the first week included Q&A sessions with a Supreme Court justice, senior members of the executive branch, and Senator Chris Coons (D-DE), the first Truman Scholar elected to the U.S. Senate. Scholars participated in a simulation of congressional decision making, a workshop about arts, culture, and public policy, and—always a highlight of the week—a meal at Ben's Chili Bowl, a much-loved DC institution.

After the orientation week, scholars begin their eight-week full-time internship placements. We do our best to match internship placements to scholars' interests. And thanks to the goodwill formed by the foundation's track record of providing agencies and organizations with first-rate people over the years, our scholars tend to obtain more substantive opportunities—and have more positive experiences—than many others who intern in DC.

During the period of their internships, we bring the scholars together every Tuesday evening for workshops planned by the scholars on a rotating basis on topics related to their professional development. We also hold occasional social gatherings throughout the summer, and the scholars tend to plan many more on their own—potlucks, happy hours around the city, and road trips on the weekends. We end the summer with a half-day symposium where scholars present to one another about their summer experiences.

We consistently hear from Truman Scholars that their participation in Summer Institute is the highlight of their Truman experience. Many come into Summer Institute with no interest in living or working in Washington, DC, over the long term; others see their arrival in Washington as the beginning of something permanent. By the end of the summer, at least as many from the former group have joined the latter as the other way around. Summer Institute is a structured opportunity for Truman Scholars to experiment professionally and grow personally.

One Truman Scholar who recently participated observed:

> *My summer in DC proved to be a tremendous growth and networking opportunity. As a scholar placed at the Department of Health and Human Services' Office of Health Affairs, I was involved in a study of state animal disease response plans. My supervisors were a fantastic set of veterinarians with unique professional experiences who encouraged me to engage in other DHS and federal operations, opening my eyes to an entirely new sector*

of endless career potential. Summer Institute supplemented this phenome-
nal internship by providing interactions with outstanding leaders in other
fields. I also grew closer to my fellow scholars and was humbled by their
extraordinary successes. Because of Summer Institute, I entered veterinary
school with an entirely new perspective on public practice and policy.

This scholar was one of the first in the foundation's history to pursue a degree in veterinary science. Her choice of that graduate program and her understanding of how it connected to public service were influenced by her participation in Summer Institute. That is a home run in our book.

Even for those who either do not end up liking their internship placement or find that Washington, DC, is not the place for them, the experience of being with other Truman Scholars is memorable, leaving them with lasting friendships. From the foundation's perspective and from a professional perspective, it can be as worthwhile for scholars to figure out what is not for them as it is for them to determine the paths to pursue.

Building Community for Public Service Leadership

By design the Truman Scholarship provides money for graduate education. But we do not want Truman Scholars going to graduate school until they have confidence about how a specific program and degree will help them in their careers. The Summer Institute is designed to help move Truman Scholars down the road to where they have clarity about the type of graduate program that is right for them. Sure, the application for the Truman Scholarship has a few questions about what graduate program the applicant will attend and what jobs he or she will seek in public service. But we find that most Truman Scholars who look back five years later have not followed the path outlined in their applications, and that is just fine with us. We use the answers to those questions to assess how candidates think about their future, not to nail them down to an unalterable professional track.

Our experience at the foundation suggests that scholars (1) select more appropriate graduate programs, (2) do better in graduate school, and (3) remain in public service longer if they have taken time off to work and/or intern after completing their undergraduate degrees. Summer Institute encourages that break between college and graduate school. About one-quarter of each class of Summer Institute scholars receives offers to stay in their placements for a full year following the summer. And the overwhelming majority of Summer Institute scholars report deeper friendships and stronger connections with their fellow Truman Scholars as a result of spending the summer together in Washington. They form bonds, both professional and personal, that remain meaningful and important throughout their careers.

Summer Institute is not for everyone, and all Truman Scholars do not participate in it. Some have other plans for the summer after they graduate, and we certainly do not require the program. During the Truman Scholar selection process, a student's interest in Summer Institute has no effect on his or her likelihood of being selected. From one year to the next, we find that roughly three-quarters of each cohort participate, and those who do so enjoy their time in Washington.

The environment for public service leadership has substantially changed since the Truman Scholarship Foundation was created. Public trust in government has plummeted over the past thirty-five years, and the shift in public attitudes makes the challenges to morale for those who aspire to be leaders in public service more acute. The Summer Institute and other programming by the foundation seek to build community among scholars—within their yearly cohorts and across the thirty-five classes of Trumans—in ways that mitigate the effects of this difficult environment on personal and professional goals. In fact, for many Truman Scholars programs like the Summer Institute are more important than the scholarship money, and that makes our investment in programming worth every penny spent.

3

Enough about Me, What Do You Think about Me?
Surviving the Truman Interview

TARA YGLESIAS

Tara Yglesias has served as the deputy executive secretary of the Truman
Foundation for the past eight years and has been involved in the selection
of Truman Scholars since 2001. During this time she had the opportunity
to study the trends and characteristics of each incoming class of scholars. She
used this knowledge to assist in the development of new foundation programs
and initiatives, as well as the design of a new foundation website and online
application system. An attorney by training, she began her career by spending
six years in the office of the public defender in Fulton County, Georgia.
She specialized in trial work and serious felonies but also assisted with the
training of new attorneys. A former Truman Scholar from Pennsylvania, she
also served as a senior scholar at the Truman Scholars Leadership Week and
the foundation's Public Service Law Conference prior to joining the
foundation's staff.

Few things can derail an accomplished candidate or an otherwise reasonable faculty advisor quite like an interview experience that turns out to be unsuccessful. This disappointment is acute and often lasting. For candidates the experience can sour everything they learned during the process. For advisors an unsuccessful interview, particularly for a favored candidate, can lead to a full-blown existential crisis. The Truman Foundation often deals with the fallout from these experiences—most often in the form of faculty advisors who call us to find out what they might have done differently.

In most cases the answer is the always unfulfilling nothing. The difference between a Truman Finalist and a Truman Scholar is often one of tiny margins wholly outside the control of the advisor and, in some cases, the candidate. Understanding the uncontrollable nature of the interview process is vital to understanding both how best to prepare candidates for the experience and how to deal with the outcome.

This essay discusses the nature of the interviews, provides suggestions for candidate preparation, and offers advice for dealing with the aftermath. Though much of this material is generic to many interview situations, the lessons learned are mainly drawn from the Truman interview process.

The Interview: Fickle Food on a Shifting Plate

If a school is able to produce finalists with some regularity, the institution's Truman program is both identifying the right candidates and presenting the students in the best possible light. The Truman Foundation considers having finalists, not scholars, to be a true marker of the success of an individual institution. We realize universities may feel differently.

We make this distinction because once advisors have (repeatedly) hit the submit button on a student's application, their part in the process—the part that is controlled, monitored, and knowable—is over. Advisors can work with students to craft prose of heartbreaking quality. Recommendation letters can provide compelling and vibrant details. The Truman faculty representative can write the single-best letter of nomination ever, moving the committee to rapturous tears. Advisors can even channel Lydia Grant during mock interviews ("You want the Truman? Well, the Truman costs. And right here is where you start paying—in sweat"), but advisors are controlling only the preparation of the candidate. Preparation will go only so far and does not guarantee results.

Even the best-prepared finalist is at the whim of the inherently subjective interview process. Yes, I used the *s*-word. Although we provide our panelists with explicit instructions about our criteria, do our best to guard against interviewer bias, and endeavor to give each finalist the same consideration, the process necessarily has subjective elements.[1]

Understanding the nature of the Truman interview begins with a thorough and, likely, somewhat dull explanation of the interview process. Our panelists receive the applications about two weeks prior to the interview date. Along with the applications, we send guidance from the foundation, a list of suggested questions,[2] and a copy of our Bulletin of Information.[3] We provide a schedule and a blank form to allow the panelists to write comments or, if they wish, score the materials.

The guidance given to the panelists begins by reminding them that they are the foundation's "investment committee." The choice of words is deliberate. By naming a student as a Truman Scholar, the panelists will require the investment of a good deal of foundation resources. It may come as a surprise to those outside the process, but our panelists are not evil dream crushers. If we permitted it, our panelists would give every finalist a scholarship of some sort. We must remind them of their role and the sobering reality that they have only a few scholarships to award. We provide our panelists with guidance in their decision making, including a list of attributes that all Truman Scholars must possess.

Likelihood of becoming a change agent. The finalist should work well with others to affect public policy or to exert leadership so that others follow his or her lead.

Commitment to a career in public service. The finalist has the values, ambitions, and desires that seem likely to lead to a career in public service. The foundation defines public service as employment in government at any level, uniformed services, public interest organizations, nongovernmental research and/or educational organizations, public and private schools, and public service–oriented nonprofit organizations, such as those whose primary purposes are to help needy or disadvantaged persons or to protect the environment.

Ability to hold his or her own at the proposed graduate or professional school. A recommender could write an enthusiastic recommendation to the dean of this school. The person need not become an academic star at the institution.

Heart and compassion. The primary concern of the candidate is with the welfare of others and not with personal ego nor selfaggrandizement.

These criteria are the same as those listed on the website and drilled into our collective consciousness during any of countless NAFA appearances. The order of the criteria is significant as well; the leadership and service components are paramount.

In terms of interview guidance, panelists are asked to spend no more than five to seven minutes on the candidate's application and policy proposal. We encourage the panelists to instead ask provocative questions in the candidate's general field. Panelists are repeatedly instructed to give the students a challenging interview. Our panelists take these instructions very seriously.

We do not send along any information from our readers, the Finalist Selection Committee. The applications are transmitted to our panelists without comments or scores. Panelists are explicitly instructed to come to their own conclusions about the written materials. We also do not require panelists to score the materials, although nearly all of our panelists arrive with the applications ranked or scored in some fashion.

Prior to the 2012 cycle, panelists were notified if our Finalist Selection Committee judged an application to be outstanding. The outstanding rating was rarely given—of the 600 applications a year, fewer than ten received this designation. Based on panelist feedback, we have decided to eliminate this practice. Panelists felt that this designation put too much pressure on the performance of the applicant.

By the day of the interview, most panelists will have spent quite a bit of time pouring over the applications. They generally arrive with lists of questions and extensive notes. All are genuinely enthusiastic to meet the finalists and hand out as many Truman Scholarships as possible. The foundation's greatest challenge is to keep the panelists from handing out too many scholarships.

We begin the day with an orientation, both for the panelists and the finalists. The panelist orientation usually is quite short, with a member of the foundation's staff going over the marching orders for the day. Many of our panelists are veterans of the process, either as panelists or as Truman Scholars. Much of the panel's orientation time is spent catching up on old friends rather than actively planning how to make a finalist's life miserable.

The orientation with the finalists takes a bit longer.[4] The panelists introduce themselves and go over the schedule for the day. As someone focused on process, I review the entire day in what can be described only as a comic level of detail. Sharing specific and extensive information about the interview process with all finalists is another attempt to level the playing field. We do not want a student who comes from a school without a robust Truman program to spend his morning fretting over whether he will have water while a student from a school with an established Truman program comfortably reads affirming text messages from her faculty advisor. We accept that there will always be inequalities, but access to information about our process should not be one of them.

After whipping the finalists into a frenzy of anticipation, the panelists adjourn to begin the interviews. Prior to a candidate's interview, we may discuss his or her application generally. We usually settle on a first question or, at least, a person who is tasked with the first question. From there the interview is entirely unscripted. We do not settle on an order of questions. We do not discuss who is going to ask questions about which topics. We just see where the interview takes us.

This may cause some finalists and their advisors to recoil in horror—because this part is where things get fuzzy. The flow of the interview depends on both the mood of the panel and the response of the person being interviewed. This statement seems obvious, but understanding and accepting this point is critical to understanding the interview process and preparing students to effectively present themselves.

We have only twenty minutes with each finalist, so when the student gets into the room, we go right to work. Although some panels and certain panelists will lob a "how are you?" at a finalist, usually we immediately start with substantive questions. The types of questions greatly vary with different panels and individual panelists, but there are a few constants.

We spend very little time rehashing materials in the application (e.g., can you describe exactly how you cured malaria?). If we do ask these types of questions, they are likely needed to clarify something in the application and will be dealt with quickly.

There are no trick questions. We want to hear the finalists' answer, not what they think we want to hear. Panelists will often play devil's advocate (and occasionally *devil's* devil's advocate). There is no way to guess how a panelist might personally feel about an issue, and the next panelist might feel another way entirely. Truman interviews are about understanding the passion of the finalist, not about exploring the views of the panelists. Finalists should just answer the question.

There are no wrong answers, even if the answer is actually wrong. Many successful Truman Finalists have answered questions inarticulately, incompletely, or incorrectly. The Truman interview is not a dissertation defense. We do not expect a finalist to know everything about an issue. Answering "I don't know" is appropriate (indeed, preferred) when the finalist finds herself on thin intellectual ice.

We do not (usually) mind when finalists change the subject. Panels will sometimes get on to a topic and not let it go. It is appropriate to respond to a question and then use the response as a way to redirect the conversation. If panelists are not finished with a topic, they are quick to let students know.

Questions cannot be interpreted as anything other than questions. Some finalists spend a lot of time rehashing the interview and trying to draw conclusions from the questions asked ("They asked only one question about my policy proposal. They hate me!"). The type and the variety of questions mean nothing.

At the eighteen-minute mark (a bit earlier if a finalist tends to have long answers, a bit later if the answers were shorter), a panelist will announce that it is the last question. After finalists respond to the last question, they will be permitted to close the interview on their own terms. Although the finalists know this portion of the interview is coming, it still seems to throw several of them into a panic. There are a few things to keep in mind about the closing statement.

A good, bad, or indifferent closing is not going to change the outcome. Finalists have delivered dreadful, lengthy, quote-filled soliloquies and still won. Others have moved me to the point where I actually thought about being moved to tears and did not prevail. Most finalists, win or lose, offer just fine closing statements. The only thing the closing statement can do is make the student feel good (or not) about the experience.

It should not be a "statement." Brief and in keeping with the tone of the interview is the best policy. A student may be relieved that she made it through *The Rime of the Ancient Mariner* by memory, but we probably did not radiate good vibes on her way out.

It can simply be, "Thanks! This was fun!" Some of the most success-ful statements are those in which finalists thank the panel, honestly say whether it was as bad as they expected, and reflect on that moment.

Questions or suggestions are best saved for later. Some students have turned around and asked the panel a question. This tactic never goes well, as the thunderous confused silence seems to chase the finalist right out the room. Others have used the time to suggest ways for the process to be improved. Since many of the panelists have only limited exposure to the inner workings of the application process, well-meaning suggestions are often met with brow furrowing and panicked glances. Again, asking questions is not the best way to close an interview.[5]

Finalists should not cry. This is not because it has an impact on a finalist's application in any way but because it makes everyone deeply uncomfortable.

After the candidate leaves, we briefly talk about him while he is still fresh in our memory, usually mentioning a few strengths or things to con-sider. After this quick chat, we move to the next finalist. It is impossible to tell how a finalist fared from the length of the break after the interview. Some Truman winners have left the panel speechless. Some finalists who were not successful have also left the panel speechless, albeit in a different way. Sometimes we are running late or are subject to external pressures (lunch delivery time, early flights).

Once we have interviewed every finalist from a state (the goal is to have a scholar from each state), we usually have a bit more time to discuss the finalists. This discussion may take place at the end of the day or dur-ing lunch, depending on the schedule. The discussion is sometimes over quickly, but more often it is wide-ranging, long, and bloody.

Oddly, the actual decision usually is the easy part. Most often, a clear Truman emerges from the fray. When no clear winner is apparent, we usually are deciding among two or three front-runners. The discussion can focus on many things: the student's performance in the interview, his written record, and the likelihood he will go into public service. Any item in the application or in the interview is fair game for discussion and consideration.

The discussion does not focus, however, on the institution the student attends. Panelists do not consider the performance or the reputation of the school. The panelists do not know whether a school has other finalists in contention. The decision must be made based on the record of the finalist alone. The only time the school is discussed is in the context of what opportunities were available to the student.

In rare cases we may request a second interview. The second interviews happen at the end of the day and are very short, usually only a few questions. Second interviews are sometimes used when the panel cannot resolve a conflict without the input of the finalist, when the panel cannot determine which of two candidates should be selected as the scholar, or when a finalist freezes or breaks down during the interview. Finalists should not worry about second interviews, since they are so rare.

In order for a scholar to be named, the entire panel must agree. We do not permit three-to-two votes. If the panel cannot come to an agreement, then that state might not have a scholar that year. Once a decision is made on each state, we go through the same process to determine whether an at-large recommendation can be made. The at-large scholar can come from any of the states interviewed that day. Under normal circumstances only especially large regions are guaranteed at-large scholars, but we do have the flexibility to award at-large scholarships in any region should a strong case be made. Scholars will never know if they are selected at-large, and the distinction between the state scholars and the at-large scholars vanishes as soon as the selection cycle is complete.

But what makes the difference between a Truman Finalist and a Truman Scholar? In the vast majority of interviews, the finalist did not say or do something wrong so much as the scholar said or did something right. One person will have a day when her hair is perfect, the train is on time, the coffee shop gives her a discount for no reason, and she finds a forgotten twenty-dollar bill in her pocket. The other will have one in which his shoelace rips, he arrives at the stop to watch the bus pull away, he drops everything he touches, including his coffee, and he finds a forgotten leaky pen in his pocket. A million little things may impact a student's performance, and they are entirely outside anyone's control.

Even if a finalist attempts to control for luck—she shaves her head, sleeps at the interview site, forgoes coffee, and keeps pens only in little plastic baggies—she must now face the whims of the panelists. The panelists must negotiate their own interests and biases during the process. To account for bias, the Truman Foundation tends to gravitate toward lawyers and judges as panelists since they have practice putting aside their feelings. Although the panelists do an excellent job of putting aside their ideological, political, and personal beliefs, they still are people who ultimately make decisions based on who and what they like. One panelist's charming may be another person's smarmy; one panelist's delightfully restrained may be another panelist's off-puttingly aloof.

Although advisors cannot control the panel's perception of their candidates, they can control the information that we consider. In their letters of nomination, advisors should add context that helps the panel have the best possible interview with the student. If a finalist is slow to warm up, tell us. If a student speaks slowly, let us know. We moderate our approach given what information is implicit in the application, but explicit information would help even more. At the very least, advisors should not oversell a finalist's personality in the letter of nomination. Quiet and thoughtful is fine—and is often a Truman—but not if we were told to expect a firecracker.

Preparation: Fight the Battle before it Begins

Much ink, bandwidth, and advisor brainpower has been spilled over how best to prepare students for an interview. We see countless different methods and levels of preparation. Panicked advisors contact the foundation convinced they are not doing enough or are doing too much. Given the variety of preparations made by different institutions, the best advisors can do is prepare their students enough but no more.

Although readers might shudder and demand to be told how many mock interviews to do, the level of preparation needed depends on the student. Some need more preparation just to be comfortable; some need less preparation so as not to appear artificial. By the time advisors (repeatedly) submit a student's materials, they should have some idea of his personality and comfort level with the interview process. Instincts about how much preparation a student needs are important to develop.

We recommend that students have at least one mock interview. The content of the mock interview is not nearly as important as just having the experience. Most students have not had the pleasure of having five slightly frightening, very impressive people peppering them with questions. Many students have not been asked to sit still in a suit for more than five minutes. Practicing both is a good way to prepare for the Truman.

When creating the mock interview, consider the tenor of the Truman interview. Interviews are rigorous—sometimes, they can even feel hostile—but they do tend to be conversational. The interactions between the panelists and the finalist are a bit more casual than some other interview settings. Our panelists are sometimes intentionally funny. Train finalists how to read an interviewer for social clues. Students should know that it is okay to laugh at a joke or a lighthearted comment. They can relax into a conversational mode if that feels comfortable and seems appropriate. It is not a good idea for finalists to be more casual than the panel, but it is equally unwise to be much more formal. Good preparation helps students to understand how to negotiate this conundrum.

Covering logistics is helpful, too. Finalist often are anxious about things that seem silly but loom large as the stress of the interview draws near.

Does the dinner on the night before the interview count? These dinners do not count, but they can help a finalist have a better interview. The panelists and the foundation's staff do not attend these dinners. They are organized and hosted by the Truman Scholars Association. We do not receive a report from the dinners. Students who attend and meet fellow finalists, however, seem more at ease the next day. This level of familiarity allows students to have a better interview.

Do I need to bring anything to the interview? All students should bring identification. We do not ask for original documents or additional materials. Finalists may wish to bring a copy of their application to review prior to their interview. Finalists should also bring something to entertain and distract them while they are waiting. A deck of cards is a good choice for the more gregarious and quaintly antique finalist; a laptop and headphones are an excellent choice for the more introverted.

Can I bring things into the interview room? Finalists seem, for some reason, to want to bring things into the interview room. Generally, this practice is not recommended. Bringing additional items into the interview room seems to distract the finalist. Conversation grinds to a halt while a student jots down notes with a pad and a pen. An overfull water bottle goes horribly awry. Things in the interview room also tend to distract the panel. One young lady insisted on bringing her overstuffed purse into the room, and several panelists could not stop staring at its bulging contents. She ultimately won, but she had to overcome her purse.

Students should surrender to the interview experience. The root cause of many unsuccessful Truman interviews has to do with the student failing to demonstrate her personality, or any personality, during the interview. I doubt any advisor is telling students, "Go in there and be as dull as possible!" But sometimes that is what happens. Some of the lack of personality may be due to nerves, but some of it appears to be the result of a notion that being perfect is infinitely better than being interesting. We prefer finalists with texture—and flaws.

Too many mock interviews, or too much repetition of questions, tends to create a robotic response from the finalist. Finalists will fall madly in love with a turn of phrase and wedge it into conversation whenever possible. Varying the way questions are asked and discouraging students from relying on canned—or even partially canned—responses will help them avoid this trap.

Sharing the interview experiences of former finalists is fine, but exercise caution. We know that certain schools keep dossiers on questions we have asked and have extensive debriefs with those who have interviewed. This practice has not proven to be especially helpful. In some cases, students have become increasingly nervous when their information turned out to be inaccurate ("Wait. The panelists are being nice to me. I must really be doing a bad job! They hate me!"). Experiences are unique to that finalist at that time. Avoid relying on the experience of one person.

Likewise, gathering information about the panelists is not particularly useful, either. It is a good policy for the student to know who is going to be on their panel—members will be listed on our website.[6] All the information that the finalist is expected to know (name, title) can be found there. Finalists who obsessively Google panelists in an effort to figure out how to woo them tend to come off as slightly creepy. The only exception would be if a student was interested in an issue that falls within the purview of one of the panelists. In that case, a bit of light research may be prudent. This research should be done only to avoid the very embarrassing moment when a finalist tries to condescendingly explain how a bill becomes a law while a professional hill staffer looks on.

The Aftermath: It's All Over but the Crying

I often tell the dramatic story of my own Truman interview. The story is compelling: a plucky working-class girl who wins over the hostile panel by her sheer charm and determination. The problem is that it did not happen that way. Louis Blair (the executive secretary of the Truman Foundation for sixteen years) was on my panel, and we have discussed this many times. His recollection, which is likely correct, can do nothing to change my impression. What I remember is what really happened, truth be damned.

Finalists often return with a story. There usually is a point where it all goes wrong—a wrong answer, a suddenly hateful panelist, or conspiring fates appear from nowhere to thwart the finalist in her quest. But much like the apocryphal tale of my own interview, Truman interviews don't happen this way. Finalists do not lose a Truman over one unfortunate turn of phrase. Conversely, finalists do not win based on one clever turn of phrase—although one man came close.

This finalist was a clear front-runner on paper: his public service commitment was outstanding; his leadership skills were exceptional; and he had a compelling personal story that cemented his future goals. His interview was unfulfilling. He seemed uncomfortable and reticent. After discussing all the finalists, we kept returning to him. We felt he was closest to the Truman Scholar selection criteria, but the interview left us with questions. We decided to call him back for a second interview and asked him one question, "If you could change anything about today, what would it be?" He said that he would like to stand up. He did; we conducted a second interview; and he won. Even in this case, he was the front-runner. His defining moment merely cemented the Truman, but it did not win the day.

This story is one from thousands of interviews. The more typical but less dramatic story is one where a student's consistency wins over the panel. Finalists sometimes say truly unfortunate things during an interview; panelists sometimes let their attention wander; fire alarms sometimes go off midinterview; but a finalist cannot lose the scholarship based on one dramatic turn.

Of course, there are stories of panelists slamming shut their notebooks after a finalist answers a question carelessly or tales in which the student was doing well until he revealed he was a Democrat or a Republican or a fan of Nickleback—and then it all turned sour. My favorite, which I hear every now and again, concerns a finalist who asked me, rather unpleasantly, to get her coffee. According to the story, she was doomed from the beginning. In truth, I thought her request was more funny than insulting, and I did not tell any of the panelists about it. Her performance in the interview was shaky, and she was not able to demonstrate her passion for service as compellingly as some of the other candidates. Her love of coffee never came up.

But the repetition of these stories is disconcerting. These stories place a lot of emphasis on details that matter little. Answering questions thoroughly is important; being polite is important; concealing your questionable taste in music is imperative; but one slip should not become the focus of the experience. Finalists should not turn the interview experience, from which students might learn something valuable, into a referendum on this one moment.

In the inevitable postmortem, students should reframe the experience, thinking about what went well, what was enjoyable, and what they learned, keeping in mind that whatever the worst moment of the interview might have been, the panelists likely do not remember it. Sending thank-you notes helps diminish any lingering bad taste (like all of our panelists, I may not remember who answered a question poorly, but I do recall every thank-you note).

Regardless of the outcome, we hope that the Truman interview is a valuable experience. After each interview panel, we leave marveling at the number of high-quality applicants and lamenting our limited number of scholarships. The value of the interview is obvious to us: we are exposed to these wonderful applicants, and they are exposed to their fellow finalists. We know we cannot provide every deserving finalist with a scholarship, but we can at least introduce her to others who share her values. By understanding the nature of the interview, providing good preparation, and learning to manage the aftermath of the interview, faculty advisors can help to make sure the interview is a valuable learning experience.

4

Expanding Undergraduate Research Opportunities
Goldwater Scholarships in Mathematics, Science, and Engineering

JOHN A. LANNING AND
W. FRANKLIN GILMORE

John A. Lanning is the assistant vice chancellor for undergraduate experiences and a professor of chemistry at the University of Colorado–Denver. At Denver he directs and oversees campus-wide academic programs for the general education core curriculum, the first-year seminar program for high school students transitioning to the university, experiential learning through internships and undergraduate research, University Honors and Leadership, and Early Alert intervention for undergraduate students needing support. In 2012 Lanning was selected as an Outstanding First-Year Advocate at the First-Year Experience conference for his work with students entering the university. He established Denver's scholarship committee, which supports undergraduate students applying for national and *international scholarships, and he has served as a national scholarship reviewer for the Goldwater and Udall foundations. He received his bachelor's degree in chemistry from Iowa State University, his PhD in analytical chemistry from the University of Tennessee–Knoxville, and postdoctoral clinical research experience at The Ohio State University.*

W. Franklin Gilmore *is president of the Barry Goldwater Scholarship and Excellence in Education Foundation (BGSF). Prior to becoming president of BGSF, Gilmore was professor and chair of medicinal chemistry at the University of Mississippi, vice president and executive vice president at West Virginia Tech, and chancellor of Montana Tech. He reviewed applications for Goldwater Scholarships for twenty-two years. His vita includes a bachelor's in chemistry from VMI, a PhD in organic chemistry from MIT, a certificate from IEM at Harvard, and a postdoctoral year at Florida State.*

In 1986 as Senator Barry M. Goldwater of Arizona was retiring, the U.S. Congress appropriated money to endow the Barry Goldwater Scholarships in Mathematics, Science, and Engineering and to establish the Barry Goldwater Scholarship and Excellence in Education Foundation. The foundation was established to foster excellence in science and mathematics as a tribute to the leadership, courage, and vision of Senator Goldwater. The purpose of this independent microagency of the executive branch is to furnish a continuous supply of highly educated research mathematicians, natural scientists, and engineers to the nation.

The enabling act of Congress authorizes the award of undergraduate scholarships, graduate fellowships, and honoraria to outstanding educators, teachers, and persons who have volunteered to assist in secondary schools. Although the enabling act authorizes the foundation to offer graduate fellowships and honoraria to teachers, up to this date only undergraduate scholarships have been awarded. Since 1989 the foundation has held twenty-three competitions, through which it has selected 6,418 undergraduate scholars from 615 academic institutions representing the fifty states, the Commonwealth of Puerto Rico, and as a single entity, Guam, the Virgin Islands, American Samoa, the Trust Territories of the Pacific Islands, and the Commonwealth of Northern Marianas.

Nomination and Application

Each regionally accredited four-year college or university has the opportunity to nominate up to four outstanding sophomore or junior-level students, and each two-year college may nominate as many as two outstanding students each year. Applicants must be nominated by the institutional representative (faculty representative) named by the campus chief executive officer (president, chancellor, rector, etc.). The foundation contracts with ACT to accept, process, and review the applications. The names of institutional representatives, as well as the forms and instructions for on-line nominations and applications, are found at www.act.org/goldwater.

Statistical data for the 2012 Goldwater Scholars are presented in Tables 1 and 2. Although these data moderately vary from year to year, those for 2012 are reasonably representative of the scholars for the twenty-three competitions.

The competition to earn a Goldwater Scholarship clearly is quite competitive. An idea of just how intense the competition is can be gained from the success of Goldwater Scholars in winning other prestigious scholarships. Scholars from the twenty-three competitions have won 80 Rhodes Scholarships, 118 Marshall Scholarships, and 110 Churchill Scholarships. In 2012 six of the fourteen Churchill Scholars were Goldwater Scholars.

Table I. 2012 Goldwater Scholars

	Nominees	Scholars
Total	1,123	282
Female	43.1%	38.3%
Male	56.9%	61.7%
Sophomores	28.7%	20.6%
Juniors	71.3%	79.4%
Two-Year Colleges	2.4%	0.4%
Four-Year Institutions	97.6%	99.6%
GPA	3.8	3.96

Table 2. 2012 Goldwater Scholars' Fields of Study

Field	Number of Scholars
Computer Science	10
Engineering	
Bio or Biomedical	19
Electrical	5
Chemical	17
Other	17
Mathematics	20
Science	
Biochemistry	11
Biology	25
Chemistry	35
Physics	32
Other or Combinations	91
Total	**282**

Selection Process

Reviewers of Goldwater Scholarship applications are selected from faculty and others with broad research, teaching, and administrative experience in mathematics, science, or engineering. Reviewers also represent a variety of employers, including governmental research and granting agencies, university admissions and financial aid offices, private and public institutions, two-year colleges, four-year colleges, and four-year universities. The reviewers now include Goldwater Scholars from some of the early scholars who have advanced in their careers.

The reviewers are paired in teams to evaluate the applications. All nominees are evaluated as a group by state of legal residence regardless of the location of the institution that nominated them. For example, an institution that has a national student body might find that its four applicants were reviewed by four different teams; whereas an institution with a student body primarily from one state would likely find all of its nominees reviewed by one team. The reviewers evaluate nominees only from states where they have not gone to school or worked. Even under these guidelines, reviewers occasionally encounter a nominee of whom they have personal knowledge or with whom they have previous associations. This connection to the nominee would immediately disqualify the reviewer, and another team would review him or her.

Quotas or targets are not assigned to the states, and no emphasis is placed on selection by gender, type of institution, discipline of study within the qualifying disciplines, or financial need of the nominee. The reviewers are given the approximate number of scholars the foundation can financially support before the review begins. They know that if 1,200 students are nominated and the foundation can financially support only 300 scholars, 900, or 75 percent, of the nominees must be cut. On the one hand, a state may have ten nominees from which the reviewers find none who meets the Goldwater Scholar standards. That state would have no scholars that year, which does happen. On the other hand, a state might have four nominees of which three are selected as scholars.

The following four primary criteria are given approximately equal weight in reviewing an application: (1) academic achievement, (2) progression toward goals, (3) the research essay, and (4) letters of reference. Each criterion is discussed in the following section. The review team selects a state where neither member has a conflict of interest. Each team member independently reviews the applications and assigns either a numerical rating or a descriptive rating, such as "good" or "outstanding," for each criterion. The team members then discuss each nominee and make a decision on the scholars for that state.

The Primary Criteria

ACADEMIC ACHIEVEMENT

In this category grades are an obvious consideration. Given that straight As would merit a GPA of 4.0, the 2012 scholars had an average GPA of 3.96. Completion of or plans to complete advanced courses in either the major discipline or another discipline are definite positives. Academic awards and scholarships are also viewed as evidence of academic achievement. Please note that a 4.0 GPA does not assure a nominee's selection. Academic achievement comprises only one-quarter of the consideration given an applicant. Nominees with GPAs lower than 4.0 are selected as scholars, though they must be stronger in the other categories.

PROGRESSION TOWARD GOALS

In this category the reviewers look for evidence of professional aspirations for a research career in mathematics, the natural sciences, or engineering. Candidates who do not have a passion for a career in research should probably not be in this competition. If the career goal is to earn the MD/PhD (or another professional degree and a PhD), the need to have a medical degree in order to facilitate the type of biomedical research desired must be clearly and convincingly articulated. This also is true of other disciplines, such as engineering, when the career aspiration is professional practice as opposed to research. Throughout the application, a strong and consistent case must be made for a career in research.

All activities in which the nominee has participated will be considered under this category. The reviewers evaluate nominees' research, their other extracurricular activities (e.g., athletics, the arts, student government), and their statements of career goals. Although a completed research project is a definite plus, candidates for this competition are not required to have performed research. Nominees who have not started research should discuss a well-focused project in which they would like to be involved. Nominees with research experience should cite evidence of publications, manuscripts in progress or at press, posters presented, or oral presentations of the research and specify their role in the project, including their role in preparing the manuscript or the presentation. Class projects that involve laboratory work should not be listed as research.

THE RESEARCH ESSAY

The ideal essay is one written by the nominee reporting on a research project she or he has completed. The essay should be written as if it were an article to be published in a scientific periodical and read by a professional audience. Methodology that is well documented in the literature should be referenced and not described in detail in the essay.

The first page should be devoted to describing the project and its essential methodology, and the second page should be devoted to the results, including the data collected, and to an analysis of the results, including the data and the significance of the findings. If the research project is under way but not completed, the first page should be similar to that for a completed project. The second page should discuss the work that has been completed, followed by what data have been collected and what will be collected. The final part should discuss how these data will be analyzed.

Nominees not having completed or initiated a research project should select a topic about which they are passionate and describe a possible project and the method of conducting the research. The scientific question to be addressed by the research should be clearly defined, and the description of the research to be done should specify how the work will answer this question.

LETTERS OF REFERENCE

Judicious selection of the three faculty members who will write letters of reference is critical. Their relative professional stature is not as important as their knowledge of the candidate and their ability to discuss her or his potential for a research career. If the candidate has done research, the research mentor should write one of the letters. A letter writer could address a nominee's potential by favorably comparing the candidate with other students who have earned doctoral degrees and then begun successful research careers.

Too frequently, letters appear generic, slightly changed to fit a candidate. Though reviewers try not to penalize the student for these inadequacies, these generic letters or letters written for other programs and changed to somewhat fit the Goldwater program do not well serve the student. Letters of reference should be written to specifically address the characteristics of the nominee that qualify her or him to be a Goldwater Scholar.

DISCRETIONARY CREDIT

The reviewers are allowed to award very limited credit if the nominee has had to overcome extraordinary adversities or has extraordinary achievements. This credit, if awarded, is based on what the nominee writes under the heading "Personal Information" or what the institutional representative writes in the nomination part of the application.

Nomination

The application for a Goldwater Scholarship requires that the institutional representative complete and sign only the "Nominator" part of the application. The nominator is permitted, however, to make comments at the end of the nomination form. The space is currently limited to 1,500 characters, and this option is not intended to be a fourth letter of reference or a summary of the three letters of reference. Reviewers see nominators' comments, and these comments provide an opportunity to present information that was unavailable to the letter writers or about which the nominee was uncomfortable writing. Nominators also use this space to explain extenuating circumstances appropriate to the application. The intent in providing this limited space is to allow the institutional representatives the flexibility to write anything they deem appropriate for this applicant. The nominee is not penalized if nothing is written in this space. The nominator is encouraged, though, to use this space constructively. It may help, and it will not hurt.

Postreview Processing

The applications are reviewed in mid- to late February. After the review a list of the recommended scholars and a list of those recommended for honorable mention are provided to the board of trustees of the Barry Goldwater Scholarship and Excellence in Education Foundation for consideration at a meeting usually held in the middle of March. Appointment of scholars and those to be awarded honorable mention is not firm until the board approves the recommendation of the review committee. The board's decision is final. After the board approves a list of scholars and a list of those to be awarded honorable mention, ACT posts both lists on the Goldwater website. This posting usually takes place during the last few days of March. Scholars and those awarded honorable mention are sent a congratulatory letter from the chair of the board of trustees, a frameable certificate, and instructions for receiving payment of the scholarship.

Goldwater Scholarships are directly paid to the student by the U.S. Treasury through a deposit in the student's bank account as a lump-sum annual payment. To receive payment, the scholar must accept the scholarship, complete an information form, and execute a request for payment signed by the financial officer of the institution. Sophomore scholars need to send a second request for payment for their senior-year payment.

The stipend is set by the board of trustees at a maximum of $7,500. The enabling legislation specifies that costs to be considered include tuition, fees, books, and room and board. The foundation will pay only the amount of the cost of these items that exceeds the value of other scholarships. Approximately half those awarded Goldwater Scholarships receive less than the maximum stipend, and usually ten to fifteen scholars receive no financial support. They are happy to receive the honor of being designated a Goldwater Scholar. In 2012 the average stipend for the 320 scholars (281 new scholars plus the carryover sophomores) was approximately $6,400.

Feedback on Unsuccessful Applications

Upon request, the foundation will provide institutional representatives feedback on unsuccessful applications. In those cases where a sophomore applicant is not successful and where the applicant has continued to improve the depth and the quality of the credentials important to the Goldwater Scholarship competition, this feedback may be helpful in preparing an application for renomination. This feedback may be especially important to those sophomore nominees who earn the designation of honorable mention and whom the institution wishes to renominate.

5

Preparing Students to Apply for Competitive Law Schools

RICHARD MONTAUK

Richard Montauk is the author of How to Get into the Top Law Schools, *5th ed. (2011), and* How to Get into the Top MBA Programs, *6th ed. (2012). He received a bachelor's degree from Brown University, a master's in government from Harvard University, and a master's in finance and a JD from Stanford University. Early in his career he worked as a corporate lawyer for Latham & Watkins and then as a corporate strategy consultant for Bain & Co. He was a recipient of a Rotary Graduate International Ambassadorial Scholarship to study Common Market law, as it was then known, at the London School of Economics and the Institute of Advanced Legal Studies in London. He is a frequent presenter for the Association of MBAs (London), the National Association of Prelaw Advisors, the Law School Admissions Council, and leading universities regarding law and business school admissions and early career strategy.*

A book about fellowship advising may seem an odd place for an article about law school admissions, yet the topic is highly relevant to those who advise students about postgraduate scholarship opportunities. Some fellowships advisors perform double duty as prelaw advisors; others have prelaw advisors report to them. Of course, many fellowship applicants ultimately head to law school or actively consider doing so, both those who fail to win the fellowship of their dreams and those who succeed, including those who target the academic fellowships and those who target the service-oriented fellowships.

The similarities between the law school application process and that of major fellowships are substantial, particularly where the leading law schools are concerned. Both value applicants who are bright, have performed well in demanding college courses, have had an impact on others outside the classroom, and have the drive to make the most of future opportunities. Both admissions offices and scholarship reviewers prefer applicants who have considered where they are headed and the best route to get there in light of their own values, interests, skills, and goals. The process by which they are selected involves submission of personal statements and other essays, multiple recommendations, résumés, and a possible interview.

This article examines both the law school application process and how best to advise prospective applicants to the top law schools. It assumes that readers have had experience with competitive application processes and, therefore, already understand application basics such as the writing of essays and the sourcing of recommendations. It begins, however, by suggesting that many potential law school applicants should be discouraged from applying—at least without substantial self- and career exploration.

A Fateful Decision

Some fellowship applicants hope to avoid committing to a specific career by winning a grant that will underwrite further study or work while they figure out what they want to do in life. Many of these applicants will fail to win such a grant, but whether they win is unlikely to harm them in the long run. Those who win will gain some time to consider their futures (armed with the prestige of their grant) and additional knowledge and skills while remaining young enough to commit to their chosen profession in the future. Those who fail to win may learn something valuable about themselves and the world. Those who apply to law school without being sure that law is the right field for them may not be so lucky.

The practice of law is an honorable and worthwhile profession that can be very satisfying for those with the right mix of values, interests, skills, and goals, a mix that will differ according to the specific legal field, employer, and location chosen. Far too many people apply to law school, however, because they think there is a fortune to be made or, *faute de mieux,* because they cannot figure out what else to do. Recent stories highlighting graduates mired in massive law school debt and unable to secure jobs, or jobs that pay well, may discourage the former from applying. The latter—those who opt for law school as a default choice—are likely to be more of a problem.

A large minority, perhaps even a majority, of those who attend the top law schools end up regretting going to law school.[1] Many try hard to get out of practicing law but find it difficult to do so. Those most likely to find the practice of law a poor fit are those who entered law as a default option rather than as an affirmative choice. This is particularly true of those heading to law school straight from college. Not working in a white-collar environment, on a paid basis, for even a few years before law school means that many less-experienced students lack an understanding of what sort of job would actually suit them best. They tend to be surprised by how detailed legal work is, how hard lawyers work, and how very hard it is to do detailed legal work with appropriate concentration for long hours. They are famously surprised by the lack of glamour in a field that is portrayed as intensely so in nearly every film, television program, and novel that formed their understanding of it.

Misconceptions about Law and Law School

A JD IS A GENERAL-PURPOSE DEGREE

A JD was once considered the most flexible of degrees insofar as it prepared students to do almost anything. This is a silly notion. A legal education does not teach students how to develop and implement an idea for a new business, administer an ongoing business or governmental department, drum up support for a nonprofit, or master information technology.

The true multipurpose degree of today is the MBA, the skills from which would indeed help someone working in most fields.

IT IS EASY TO GET OUT OF LAW ONCE YOU ARE IN IT

Law students are often told that whether they enjoy law school does not have much to say about whether they will enjoy practicing law. There is enough truth in this that law students continue to graduation and then enter practice. Once in practice, they learn that the first few years are a form of boot camp that bears little relation to what life is like as a partner. Although many lawyers sense that they have entered the wrong field, they generally are too goal oriented to opt out early on. Only after a half dozen or more years do such lawyers finally admit they made the wrong career choice.

Law represents a decade's commitment or more. At the end of that decade, many unhappy lawyers have not yet done the hard work of assessing themselves and sufficiently exploring the world of work in order to know what they should be doing instead of practicing law. Trying to come to grips with these things in one's thirties rather than one's early twenties is difficult. Mortgage payments and an established identity as a lawyer, to name just two factors, are complications that make radical career reassessment a nightmare. In addition, nonlegal employers are not desperate to hire lawyers at high pay for nonlegal positions.

NONLEGAL EMPLOYERS HIGHLY VALUE LEGAL TRAINING

Employers value legal training only in lawyers or in fields, such as legal reporting, very closely related to law. High-tech firms, traditional companies, and everyone else in business (and in innumerable other areas, as well) often do not believe that lawyers have been taught how to think. Nor do they necessarily find that lawyers have acquired nonlegal skills worth paying for. Indeed, employers view lawyers as overly contentious, not team oriented, and narrowly focused.[2] Employers grant that lawyers (from top schools, at least) are probably pretty smart and willing to work hard. They may also consider them damaged goods, however, running away from law rather than toward something else in particular. They may also assume that because lawyers have little relevant background when choosing another field, they will likely make another poor career decision.

Initial Advice for Potential Applicants

To avoid this nightmare, those considering law school should engage in the following before committing to law: (1) evaluating their values, interests, skills, and goals with as much expert input as possible; (2) studying the work of lawyers and the various practice areas of law; (3) shadowing one or more lawyers for as long as possible; (4) working for some time in a legal environment, whether as a paralegal or in another capacity, and exploring the ways different specialties call for different skills, work rhythms, and personality types; and (5) seriously exploring nonlegal options.

Evaluative Criteria

The top law schools, like competitive fellowships, want to attract the best and the brightest applicants. Law school admissions decisions are, though, in some key respects very different from fellowship decisions. Law schools know that the composition of their incoming class will affect the all-important *U.S. News & World Report* ranking of their school, which in turn will affect their ability to attract top students (and professors and alumni donations). These rankings largely depend upon the LSAT scores of incoming students, the opinions of others in the profession, and to a lesser extent, the GPAs of incoming students, the amount of money the school spends, graduates' success in getting jobs, and various other factors. The two factors that admissions deans and committees can control to some extent are the LSAT and the GPA numbers. Because admissions deans now understand that the LSAT scores matter much more than GPA numbers in the rankings, LSAT scores count for much more in admission decisions. There are a few basic rules for who gets accepted.

Applicants with stellar academic and LSAT results are accepted. This is done implicitly on a niche-by-niche basis, with underrepresented minorities, for instance, battling one another for seats in the class rather than battling everyone in the applicant pool.

Others with compelling rationales for admission are accepted. These include applicants with strong postcollege work histories and, to a lesser extent, those with strong extracurricular and community performance or notable personal stories.

Once the bulk of a class has been admitted, admissions deans see what they have wrought. They consider the class's current LSAT and GPA twenty-fifth and seventy-fifth percentiles and the extent to which those numbers can be pushed up or dragged down by the last admits they make.

The last seats may be almost exclusively filled on the basis of LSAT or GPA data or with little regard for it. In any given year, some schools will have some seats open to those who are desirable in spite of their LSAT scores or GPAs, but the identity of those schools is not knowable in advance.

Of course, some schools are more open than others to talent that is not expressed largely in LSAT scores. A brief look at the class composition of Harvard and Stanford, for instance, suggests that the former values LSAT scores much more than does the latter.

Early Decision

Many law schools, aping their college cousins, have instituted early decision programs that promise candidates who apply in October (or November) a decision on their application by sometime in December. They do not promise candidates a substantially increased chance of admission, but this is implicit insofar as candidates generally remember that college early decision programs offer a huge admissions advantage. The admissions advantage of law school early decision programs is, however, negligible. Most candidates, especially college seniors struggling to pull together their applications, are best advised not to try to meet these early decision deadlines.

Maximizing Credentials

ACADEMIC RECORD

The ideal undergraduate record would exhibit all of the following: (1) strong academic preparation at a school known for academic rigor; (2) a demanding course load (i.e., not the path of least resistance); (3) advanced work in a second field unrelated to the major; (4) high grades throughout with few courses taken pass/fail, especially in the junior and the senior years; (5) courses requiring substantial reading, strong writing ability, good research skills, and analytical prowess; and (6) courses developing useful, substantive knowledge for the chosen future legal field.

Admissions officers view a candidate's undergraduate record as a key indicator of her intellectual ability and her willingness to work hard, making this a proxy for her academic potential in law school. The less work experience she has, the more important her college record will be.

Those with a spotty undergraduate record may improve it by taking continuing education or graduate courses. Law schools substantially differ, however, in their willingness to consider postcollege academics. They generally find it difficult to interpret the grades received because they tend not to know much about the courses and the programs involved. They do not know, for instance, the quality of the students in them, the workload required, or the grading policies applied. Someone who wishes to profit from postbaccalaureate academic work should confront these issues via an appropriate recommendation or essay.

EXTRACURRICULAR AND COMMUNITY ACTIVITIES

Extracurricular and community activities are important to admissions officers for many reasons. First, they help show how a candidate interacts with others on a regular basis. Law schools generally prefer sociable types (especially leaders) to loners, although most schools will take some candidates who appear a bit antisocial if they are strong enough in other regards. Extracurricular and community activities also show how a candidate chooses to spend her time away from school and work; demonstrate leadership, initiative, special talents, and honed skills; provide evidence of personality and character traits; and complement ideas presented within the academic profile about how the candidate will fare in a law career. In sum, they give admissions officers an idea of how someone might contribute to the law school community if accepted. Extracurricular achievement thus is particularly important for those with little or no work experience.

A law school would much rather see that a candidate put many hours of valuable effort over several years into two activities than joined every group in college, playing very limited roles. Law school admissions officers do not share the view that quantity has a quality all of its own. In fact, a long list of activities merely dilutes the overall impression that the nonacademic profile gives an admissions officer and could encourage or elicit skepticism about one's candidacy.

The particular activities in which a candidate chooses to participate generally are much less important than is the impact she has on others and on herself. Notable exceptions to this rule concern community service. A commitment to community service is especially important if someone comes from a wealthy or even moderately well-off family and has never had to work for paid wages. Similarly, those who intend to be a public interest lawyer or are applying to a public interest program will be viewed with suspicion if they have not been involved in substantial community activities. Those who come from low-income families or are required to work a great deal to help support others will not be expected, however, to have donated their limited free time to charitable efforts.

LSAT

The leading law schools regard the LSAT as a critically important part of an application. Some care more than others, however, with those schools that recently suffered a drop in their *U.S. News & World Report* rankings generally caring the most. LSAT scores tend to be more important for some candidates than for others. The younger a candidate, the more likely it will count heavily, partly because such a candidate offers fewer ways to evaluate her abilities. Someone who has a decade's work experience, for instance, offers more ways to evaluate her than does a college senior.

Furthermore, candidates in different parts of the applicant pool face different expectations regarding their LSAT scores. As a rule of thumb, African Americans' scores average ten points below those of Asian Americans and Caucasians; Hispanics', five points; and American Indians', three to five points. Thus, schools' LSAT averages must be interpreted in light of individual circumstances. An African American with a score equal to a school's twenty-fifth percentile, for instance, is likely to benefit from the score rather than be harmed by it.[3]

In the past, schools were more or less required to average a candidate's multiple scores. Law schools are now free—due to a change in their reporting requirements—to average them or take the highest (or lowest) as they choose.[4] Many still average scores, but an increasing number take the highest, especially if a plausible explanation for doing so is on offer. Some argument thus exists for taking the exam more than once in order to get the highest-possible score. Most candidates dislike the exam so much, however, that they should be urged to prepare well, take it once, and get on with life.

Those who seek to take the exam with some sort of accommodation (especially if they seek extra time) should be warned that the accommodation process is onerous and lengthy. Those who seek accommodation in the weeks rather than the (many) months before an exam are almost sure to be disappointed.

WORK EXPERIENCE

Although it is not required for applicants to have had significant work experience, more and more students are arriving at law school having already worked full time for several years or longer. Many have had accomplished careers, often entirely unrelated to the law. Law schools find this quite appealing. Northwestern, for instance, all but requires such experience of candidates. Many schools are even willing to deemphasize a less-than-exemplary academic record if an applicant has performed well in a demanding—or unusual—industry.

The amount of work experience tends to be much less important than the nature and the quality of the experience. Those whose undergraduate performances were comparatively weak should consider working a bit longer to lessen the currency of grades and course selection and to increase the amount of positive work-related information to show to the admissions committee.

The key to impressing admissions officers with work experience is not a matter of the specific job or industry. Accomplishment is the key. Admissions officers want to see people successfully take on responsibility, perform complicated analysis, wrestle with difficult decisions, and bring about change. They want people to progress in their jobs and develop relevant skills, including the ability to work with and lead others, with consequent improvements in responsibilities, salary, and title. People who meet these criteria will be highly valued no matter what industry they come from.

Note that those with weak undergraduate records or LSAT scores are more likely to improve their chances of admission at the top law schools with strong work experience than with further academic work.

Choosing Schools

The first step in choosing a school is to know well what is desired from a law degree. Someone who wants to become a partner in a megafirm in New York or London handling complicated financial transactions will presumably aim for a top-ranked school that offers a wide range of courses and a deep bench of expert professors in related fields. Note that comparably ranked schools markedly differ in their ability to deliver in different fields. For example, Yale and Stanford are both top-ranked schools of nearly identical size, yet Stanford offers more intellectual property courses than does Yale, and Yale offers more immigration law courses than does Stanford. Students with a particular interest should do their homework. Someone who hopes to practice divorce law in his hometown, however, might benefit more from a local law school with good connections to the local bar (practicing lawyers, judges, and so on).

Because of the vagaries of law school admissions, however, a candidate will probably need to apply to a substantial set of schools. All but the most highly valued applicants will need to apply to a range of schools—perhaps, across the top twenty or so rather than just the top handful. Applying to such a set of schools increases the chance not only of admission but also of getting substantial financial aid from one or more schools (see this essay's section on financing law school). A merit grant from one school can help a candidate bargain for more from a preferred school.

Presentation Strategies

Self-presentation approaches for law school applicants are similar to those for fellowship candidates. A candidate should position himself to get the fullest value out of who he is, what he has done, and where he is headed in light of what particular programs value. This positioning effort should encompass the whole of the application—the personal statement and other essays, the résumé, the recommendations, the interviews, and so on—making sure they are well integrated and consistent.

For some candidates their marketing strategy will be straightforward. Someone who worked sixty hours a week to support her ailing mother while attending college full time (and paying her own tuition) should obviously pitch herself as determined, concerned about others, and able to succeed in spite of substantial obstacles. Others may face a more difficult task of explaining who they are if their circumstances are not so stark. Nearly all candidates will benefit, however, from the use of specific themes (e.g., determination, concern about others, persistence) to focus their marketing effort. These themes will help them decide what to emphasize and what to eliminate.

Personal Statements and Other Essays

PERSONAL STATEMENTS

Leading law schools require a personal statement, generally on a topic of the candidate's choice. The choice of topic is important. Ideally, it will further the candidate's positioning effort while also showing her to be unique. As with fellowship applications, the best personal statement will be something only this candidate could write.

The general rule is that someone applying straight from college is unlikely to profit by addressing her professional goals. Admissions deans know that most collegiate applicants claim they are headed for a public interest future, yet law school career statistics show that this will be true of vanishingly few of them. In other words, youthful enthusiasm is likely to be taken as evidence of a lack of knowledge of the profession. Unless she has had substantial experience in a given field—or has been helping her parents run their law firm for the past decade—she is unlikely to be taken seriously. Instead of projecting her likely career path, a college senior should consider avenues for more fully explaining how her interests have developed over time, what she has learned about herself, what significant obstacles she has overcome, or other topics that will allow her to become more of a person to admissions officers and less of a collection of LSAT and GPA numbers.

Someone long out of college, however, almost surely should address his professional goals. A forty-year-old who writes about an epiphany he experienced in high school without explaining clearly why and how he thinks he can fashion a legal career at his age is not making the best possible case for admission.

ADDITIONAL ESSAYS

Many law schools encourage or even require that applicants submit additional essays on topics the schools have chosen in addition to a personal statement. Duke, for instance, provides an opportunity to respond to either or both of the following additional topics: "why you have chosen to apply to law school in general and Duke in particular, and/or an essay that describes how you will enhance the educational environment of the Law School and contribute to the diversity of the student body."[5] The University of Pennsylvania provides four additional topics; the University of Michigan, eight.

The opportunity (or necessity) to submit multiple essays offers a chance for applicants to more fully develop their candidacies. Strong candidates— especially those who have carefully considered why they wish to attend law school and this particular school, what career path they intend to take, and what distinguishes their candidacies—are likely to benefit from responding to such questions.

ADDENDA

Law schools generally permit candidates to submit an addendum explaining gaps or anomalies in their application. Someone whose father died during a semester when she did notably poorly should explain what happened. Similarly, someone who took the LSAT twice, receiving scores of 157 and 171, would be wise to explain why the latter is the better indicator of his academic potential. These explanations are better handled in a separate addendum rather than cluttering up a personal statement that presumably is on a different topic. In sum, the average applicant to competitive programs will probably write three essays (one personal statement and two other essays) and possibly an addendum.

Résumés

Résumés are a very important part of a law school application. A large majority of leading law schools now require one be submitted, and the remainder encourage submission. Law schools use the résumé for the following three purposes: (1) as the first item admissions officers read, a good résumé provides a quick overview of the candidate's career to date, making it easy for each succeeding piece of the file to be understood in context; (2) the résumé provides a look at the candidate's key activities in her own words and with the emphasis she considers appropriate, showing how a candidate views her efforts and achievements; and (3) the résumé makes clear the level of professionalism the candidate brings to both the application effort and her career.

There is nothing magical about one style of résumé versus another—whether the dates should be on the left or the right, for instance—but it helps to keep the following few rules in mind: (1) assume that readers may spend only thirty seconds on a résumé, and therefore, it should be only *one page,* unless someone is applying for a joint degree program (JD/PhD) that requires an academic CV; (2) use résumé-speak phrases rather than full sentences; and (3) make sure the résumé is visually appealing; it should not be so crammed with material that it is off-putting and discourages skimming or reading. The appropriate model is that of a succinct business résumé, not an endless academic one. The adolescent résumés favored by so many college seniors suggest they should be applying for babysitting or café barista jobs rather than to a professional school.

Recommendations

WHO SHOULD WRITE THE RECOMMENDATIONS?

Top law schools consider themselves to be much more academic than do preprofessional institutions (unlike most business schools). This combined with the fact that most admissions decisions are made or at least ratified by professors means that professorial recommendations carry much more weight than do workplace, community service, or extracurricular activity recommendations. This is particularly true for candidates applying straight from college.

It is highly appropriate for a candidate to submit two recommendations from professors. If a candidate has had substantial work, community service, or extracurricular experience, adding a third recommendation from someone who has overseen this experience could be of substantial value. That said, such a letter would work best if it was in addition to two professorial recommendations. Those who have been out of college for a considerable period of time may substitute workplace for professorial recommendations if necessary, but they will probably be at some disadvantage in doing so.

HOW MANY RECOMMENDATIONS SHOULD BE SUBMITTED?

Competitive law schools typically require two recommendations but permit more to be submitted. Young applicants who have not had substantial out-of-classroom experiences will probably benefit by not submitting more than two (professorial) recommendations. A third recommendation is worth adding if it adds a truly different and important perspective to your candidacy. Thus, someone who is majoring in mathematical economics and writing a thesis on Roman economic history might wish to have a professor who taught him in two economics classes and a concentrator's seminar write one letter and have his thesis advisor contribute a second. If he also pursued a minor in comparative literature, having a professor who taught him in two advanced comparative literature courses could substantially add to his profile and would be well worth submitting.

Those who have had major involvements outside the classroom are likely to benefit from having supervisors of their efforts write a recommendation. This is particularly true for those who have worked for a considerable time after college. Fewer than one in one hundred candidates are likely to benefit, however, from submitting more than four recommendations.

SPECIAL ACADEMIC CIRCUMSTANCES TO MENTION

Admissions deans are unlikely to know everything about the ins and outs of a candidate's program. Consider having a professor or a dean describe in her recommendation the nonobvious, laudatory aspects of it, especially if the candidate selected professors or courses notorious for low grades, took a particularly demanding course load, pursued a major that attracted the school's best and brightest students, wrote a thesis requiring highly problematic or in-depth research, or worked long hours (twenty-five plus per week) to pay tuition.

THE DEAN'S LETTER

A throwback to the time when college deans were expected to know a good deal about the students assigned to them, the dean's letter is still required by some law schools. They do not expect to learn much from it given that deans seldom know much of value about their students. Instead, schools generally use it to make sure applicants have not misbehaved at college, a form of disciplinary clearance.

Interviews

In the recent past very few law schools conducted any evaluative interviews of applicants. This is changing substantially. Approximately half of the top-twenty law schools now have active interviewing programs. These programs are by no means uniform, however, differing substantially in several ways.

Scope. Vanderbilt seeks, for instance, to interview all of its applicants. Harvard interviews only the finalists in its process. The University of Texas at Austin offers optional interviews available to all candidates upon request.

Format. Vanderbilt's interviews are thirty-minute in-person interviews. Harvard's are fifteen-minute telephone interviews. The University of Texas at Austin's interviews are thirty minutes long, but with a twist. Fifteen minutes are given to an applicant to make his or her pitch for admission; the other fifteen minutes are devoted to a writing exercise in which the applicant produces a sample for the school to evaluate.

Interviewer. At some schools, such as UCLA and the University of Chicago, various admissions officers conduct the interviews. At others, such as Harvard, only the admissions dean conducts interviews. At Northwestern, in contrast, admissions officers, current students, and alumni volunteers all conduct evaluative interviews.

Because numerous applicants and their advisors are unaware that many top law schools interview applicants, relatively few candidates prepare well for interviews. (A disconcerting number seem surprised by questions as predictable as, Why law? or, What kind of law most interests you and why?) Only a modest number seek out interview opportunities, giving a substantial potential advantage to well-prepared applicants who do so.

As with fellowship interviews, careful preparation can dramatically improve interview performance. The starting point of course is to assess one's candidacy in the fashion discussed in the beginning of this essay. Having done so, the next steps are to understand the differences between the programs of the various law schools and the differences in their approaches to interviewing, which are generally made clear on their websites. Applicants should be prepared to answer the following most commonly posed questions and prompts:

Tell me about yourself.
What are your greatest achievements?
What are your strengths and weaknesses?
What are your personal and professional goals?
Why do you want to go to law school?
How much do you know about the practice of law?
In what field of law do you intend to practice and why?
Where else are you applying?
Why do you want to attend this school?
How have you learned about our program?
Why should we accept you?
What would you add to the program?
Discuss [whatever legal issue is in the news].
What questions do you have?

Financing Law School

Top law schools have long expected students to incur debt to finance their degrees under the assumption that most will take high-paying jobs. The few headed for low-paying jobs in the nonprofit and governmental sectors could be helped through special law school programs to repay their loans. Both assumptions now are under pressure.

Graduates of even the top schools are no longer assured jobs in Big Law, the country's largest and highest-paying firms. Even those who land jobs in these firms are not guaranteed the $150,000-plus initial salary that was common before the 2007 market turmoil. Clients of these law firms have increasingly rejected paying for young associates at all, let alone at the high rates firms used to charge to cover the associates' high salaries. Firms have responded by reducing their hiring of graduates and paying many they do hire a much lower salary. Thus, recent hires at these firms commonly earn only $60,000 to $70,000. For those who finish law school with $130,000 or more in law school debt (often on top of $20,000 or more of college debt), debt repayment is a practical impossibility. Those earning $60,000 will probably pay taxes in excess of $20,000 and make (after-tax) debt repayments of a similar amount, leaving only $12,000 to $18,000 for all of their living expenses. This will strike many as too small a salary to warrant the time, effort, and money required to enter the profession.

Those intending to practice in the governmental, nonprofit, or small firm sectors are likely to face initial salaries of $30,000 to $65,000, with few at the high end of this range. As described, such salaries simply are too low to permit repayment of the typical debt taken on by graduates of the leading law schools. Law schools tout their loan repayment assistance programs (LRAPs), which feature debt repayment for those taking public interest jobs at modest pay. These can be lifesavers, yet all but the most generous suffer from substantial drawbacks. For instance, graduates in these programs may need to stay in a nonprofit field for ten or fifteen years to have the debt written off or have to turn down a promotion that would put them slightly above a program's income ceiling. Even worse, the flood of recent graduates into qualifying positions means that pressure on these programs' finances has increased greatly. Even some of the well-established programs may need to cut back their funding in the future.

If law students at leading schools cannot guarantee earning a hefty sum upon graduation and have reason to be nervous about whether they will be rescued by a loan repayment program, the remaining option is to reduce the cost of law school (or get rich via the lottery). Applicants seeking to reduce the amount they will pay have a number of options.

Become a resident of a state with a modestly priced but still desirable public law school. One year of working and paying taxes in a state without attending school (at least not doing so full time) is generally a sufficient period to establish residence.

Take advantage of the dog's breakfast of financial aid policies of different law schools. Some take into account, for instance, the assets and incomes of all parents (custodial or not); others consider applicants independent of their parents in determining financial aid awards.

Earn an outside fellowship to underwrite law school.

Win a merit grant from a law school (which will need to value the applicant highly to part with the money).

Chop off a semester of law school education. Recent changes in American Bar Association regulations governing law schools make it possible—with appropriate advance planning—to graduate in five rather than six semesters from some schools (those that have positively responded to the ABA's changes). This path saves approximately one-sixth of the usual tuition and allows early graduates to enter the workforce six months ahead of time and jump-start earning an income.

Some of these strategies obviously have substantial implications for one's choice of school. For instance, if someone hopes to get a merit grant from a law school, she will need to apply to schools for which she will be a notably strong candidate, which are likely to be lower ranked than those she might otherwise favor.

Conclusion

Those advising potential applicants to law school should urge them to explore whether law school and the practice of law are wise choices for them in light of their values, skills, interests, and goals, to seriously consider other fields rather than taking the lazy option of going to law school as a means of pushing real career decisions down the road, to gain relevant experience by working after college rather than immediately applying to law school, and to develop law school financing strategies appropriate to their career goals and personal circumstances. Those who do apply to law school should be urged to become the best possible candidates by developing their talents and interests while in college and thereafter and to take advantage of the multiple opportunities to stand out favorably in the application process, increasing the chance of acceptance at a leading school (and of getting the largest possible grant).

6

Welcoming African Americans to the World of International Scholarships

CAROL MADISON GRAHAM

Carol Madison Graham holds advanced degrees from Georgetown University in Middle East history and international relations. She began her involvement in international education as a U.S. diplomat. She moved to London in 1995 with her family, where she has worked in the higher education, law, and government sectors. From 2002 to late 2006, she was executive director of the US-UK Fulbright Commission. She was the first American, the first woman, and the first member of an ethnic minority to run UK Fulbright. While at Fulbright, she was very active in promoting international education opportunities for minorities and was invited by the State Department to speak about diversity issues. She also helped to create a leadership program for disadvantaged young Europeans to study in the United States. Graham writes the EngageAbroad *blog for the international exchange community and has published a study abroad prep book on the twin themes of the perception of Americans in and engaging with a foreign culture called* Coping with Anti-Americanism: A Guide to Getting the Most out of Studying Abroad. *In addition to her writing, Graham works as a consultant on cultural engagement programs for U.S. universities and serves on the boards of the Marshall scholarships, the International House Trust, and the Carnegie UK Trust.*

International scholarships have long attempted to increase the numbers of African American participants in order to better reflect the numbers of African Americans in college. According to the Institute of International Education's Open Doors data, fewer than 5 percent of study abroad students are African American.[1] After years of meager results overall, advisors are curious and a little frustrated as to why programs are not attracting many more applicants. Low numbers of African Americans applying to scholarships is not a scholarship issue alone, however, but must be seen in the wider context of study abroad. It also is of material relevance that busy fellowship and study abroad coordinators in colleges where African Americans are not in the majority may know very little about African Americans, unless they happen to be African American themselves. As a result, they may have difficulty identifying factors in the decision not to apply. As it happens, there are many reasons for African American reticence to study abroad.[2]

Historical Lack of the Travel Habit

Unless African American students have family abroad, the habit of overseas travel probably has not been a tradition in their families, reflecting a wider phenomenon in the African American community. Readers of Edith Wharton know that travel was part of the routine of the white upper class in the United States. European travel in particular was a way of establishing cultural credentials. This habit spread down through at least some of white culture, and the junior year abroad is a part of that legacy. African Americans were not a part of this cultural tradition, and with historically lower incomes and the need to keep working, they had little leisure time or money for European travel. Although lack of funds is a major and often *the* major factor in the low take up of study abroad opportunities for all students, the lack of the habit may be as powerful a disincentive for African Americans, as indicated by a student in a study abroad blog: "I can assure you that very few Black students took advantage of the opportunity, even with full financial aid. That year had more impact on my life than all my university years combined."

Language Skills

The lack of foreign-language skills also is a deterrent to applying for programs abroad. African Americans clearly share this psychological obstacle with white classmates, except that in the eighteenth and nineteenth centuries exposure to French, in particular, was seen as a sign of culture in upper-class white society. By contrast, even upper-class African Americans in the nineteenth century, with some notable exceptions such as Mary Church Terrell and W. E. B. Du Bois (both of whom studied abroad), regarded foreign-language learning as an unnecessary skill, burdened as they were with other concerns. Culture was important, but it was equated with education and habits more generally. The most influential African American educator of the nineteenth century was Booker T. Washington. His school of thought emphasized educational attainment that included practical job skills. In his autobiography, *Up from Slavery*, Washington describes a young man "sitting down in a one-room cabin, with grease on his clothing, filth all around him, and weeds in the yard and garden, engaged in studying a French grammar" as "one of the saddest things" he had seen.

Dominance of Programs to Europe

Without ancestral links to Europe, many African Americans have little interest in living in a European country, which they often (wrongly) assume will be little different from majority culture in the United States. Or they may simply be curious about other parts of the world. If programs outside Europe are not offered, many see no reason to apply.

Emphasis on Cross-Cultural Learning

For international educators the most surprising reason for the lack of interest in going abroad expressed by African Americans is the emphasis on cross-cultural learning. At first this may seem parochial, but in fact the opposite often is the case. Whereas most white Americans may know little of African American culture, the reverse is not true. A great many African Americans operate in a bicultural environment. As a minority they have their own culture, and they also participate in the majority culture. In addition to work relationships, they may have groups of white and black friends they are constantly moving back and forth between. As for African American college students, many of them have attended majority-white K–12 schools throughout and are now enrolled in a majority-white college. These students already are bicultural. So African Americans may believe that they have little to gain in cross-cultural understanding by going abroad. They are wrong in this assumption, but that does not change the fact that if we want them to apply, talking about learning to function cross-culturally may not be the best strategy.

Wrong Time Period in Career: Validation Not Study

Just because educated African Americans did not have a travel habit does not mean that they never went overseas. Traditionally, a visit abroad, mostly to Europe or Africa, was a very prestigious thing to do and seen as a validation of a significant achievement at home. Martin Luther King's travels to Europe and Africa after the Montgomery bus boycott made him world famous can be seen in this light. For many people travel abroad for study purposes is less desirable than doing so after they establish a career in which they have earned the time off and have the income to truly enjoy it. Empirical information on how studying abroad can help prepare for a career in the first place would assist advisors in moving a diversity strategy forward, in addition to the recognition of class factors.

Recruitment Strategies That Ignore Class

African Americans are no different from other Americans in downplaying the role of class, but it is there and has always been there. Recruitment attempts that fail to take class differences into consideration may also be a contributing factor in the low numbers of African Americans participating, because they unintentionally leave out some students. Lower-income African American students have a university support structure that often includes an office for minority or diversity affairs. For such students college itself can be an achievement, and such a structure provides or should provide psychological support in the event that low-income African Americans feel insecure among more well-to-do students, including other African Americans. In addition to targeting HBCUs, many national scholarship programs interact with these offices in majority-white colleges and universities to improve diversity.

Generally, higher-income African American students do not have a race-related support structure. They are more often expected to cope on their own in college. After all, many come from several generations of college graduates. This does not mean, however, that attending a majority-white university always is comfortable for them. If they have come from a tight-knit community, they too can feel at sea, sensing that the respect they are used to having as the child of a professional or a member of a social club is falling away.

For many middle-class African American students, college is more of an adjustment than they had expected. If they do feel insecure, they are not likely to seek out the office of minority affairs, which they may regard as providing support for lower-income students or carrying a racial stigma. Some African American middle-class students who do approach minority affairs offices report a lack of interest in their situations. As a result, recruitment efforts targeted at such offices risk missing these students altogether. The bottom line is that middle-class students may be apprehensive about going abroad after two years, when they have just settled into college life, for fear of reawakening the class insecurities that they may have experienced for the first time their freshman year.

Finally, for African Americans and, especially, for middle-class students, there is the parent factor. The collective experience of racial discrimination and the sacrifices of their parents create a very close relationship between African American students and their families. In order to increase interest in study abroad, colleges need to convince more parents and families that it has value. Anecdotal evidence suggests that parents whose children did study abroad, including on prestigious scholarships, either tried to dissuade them or did not understand why they found it necessary to lose focus on their education, as they saw it. Many colleges realize this but then emphasize scholarship money for international study, which sometimes misses the mark.

Middle-class families in many cases either have the money or are willing to make the sacrifice as long as they see the benefit. They are not about show me the money but about show me the career. Their history and experience have taught them to be very practical about educational opportunity, and they want to know precisely what study abroad will do to advance their children professionally. Due to the rampant discrimination of the past that made it difficult for African Americans to move into prominent positions, role models were and remain extremely important. So far middle-class role models for their children have not induced them to change their minds that study abroad is not essential to success. A prime example is the first lady.

As first lady, Michelle Obama has embraced and promoted the study abroad agenda, but many middle-class parents can be confirmed in their reticence about study abroad through her life story. They see in Michelle Obama someone like themselves, with no immigrant roots. She never took the opportunity to study overseas, although it was offered at her university, and she speaks no foreign languages. Yet she has excellent academic degrees and went on to a very respectable career before becoming internationally famous as first lady. Michelle Obama herself has told many students that she wishes she had studied abroad and had foreign-language fluency. World leaders nonetheless are clearly delighted to meet her. For the middle-class parent, she is staying true to form by traveling and meeting people abroad as a validation of her achievement. Though the first lady may indeed regret not having studied overseas, practically minded African American middle-class parents will find no flaw in her decision not to do so.

Fears of Racism

When African Americans think about living abroad, they wonder about racial attitudes in other countries. In order to put this concern into perspective, consider the vast improvement in race relations in the United States. Looking back to the past century, some of the most famous African Americans not only lived overseas but also permanently relocated there. Josephine Baker, James Baldwin, and Richard Wright all died in Paris. Although students today may not realize it, African Americans have a history of choosing to live in Europe and elsewhere. Why did this history not create an overall acceptance of studying overseas among African Americans? In part, it did not, because except for Josephine Baker (who became a star in Paris), they fell into the category of validation after fame at home. The main reason was, however, an understanding that the motivation for this exodus by famous role models was to escape the race situation in the United States. James Baldwin felt freer in Paris than in his birthplace of New York City. In addition, writers and artists who were vocal in their opposition to racism were dangerously labeled communists.

Once legal segregation was removed, the race situation improved, and the McCarthy era ended, however, African American writers and artists no longer needed to seek sanctuary abroad. The brief period of famous African Americans living abroad was regarded as more or less an aberration, and the United States seemed the best place in racial terms. Student blogs reveal that the impact their color may have on their time abroad is still of concern. According to one study of ethnic-minority students, including African Americans, who decided not to study abroad, 60 percent cited fears of racism as the main obstacle.

The following sampling of comments on student blogs reveals the ways in which students think about or experience race and studying abroad:

> *When I was out with my white friends, I was totally ignored.*

> *So, how was it being a Black American in the Middle East? Well, I'll tell you this much—skin color does matter.*

> *This is going to sound ignorant, but the reality is most minority students do not have as much interest in studying in a WHITE continent like Europe, much the same as a White student choosing to study abroad in Africa. Sure there are minorities living in Europe, but why do most schools have to always emphasize European nations to study abroad all the time?*

> *It is also worth mentioning that Neo-Nazi groups are on the rise in some communities. I was lucky and my friends told me places to avoid, etc. However, it is not always preventable. I had lit firecrackers thrown at me along with racial slurs from a group of young Neo-Nazis.*

In theory studying on an elite international scholarship should allay their fears. After all, such scholarships offer prestige, excellent student care and attention, and of course contacts that rise far above the average host country citizen. This may reassure potential applicants regarding programs outside Europe, but Europe and, especially, the United Kingdom are seen by many Americans, of all races, as overly concerned with rank and status. This may be a little frightening for African American students, including middle-class students who as previously mentioned, can be sensitive about their class status—how many times have people assumed they were poor or unsophisticated because they were black?

So what do racists abroad look like in the eyes African American students? They may look like skinheads, or they may look like the owners of Downton Abbey. Although students may be afraid of encountering physical violence or threats, they may have unspoken concerns about the disdain of strangers and of loneliness. They may also worry about social isolation from other Americans on the program.

How International Scholarships See Diversity

It is one thing for scholarship programs for Americans to encourage diversity, but how do these programs specifically address African American diversity? The answer is, with caution. It is a fact that many non-Americans do not trust the American affirmative action agenda, which in their minds (though not necessarily in their experience) risks quality for the sake of a social justice agenda. They also tend to lump diversity into the single pool of nonwhites. As far as some are concerned, they do not need to have African Americans to portray their program as diverse. Finally, they can on occasion adhere to a flavor-of-the-month mentality, just as can happen in the United States, focusing on African Americans now but Latinos or another group later without a sustained effort to build up a particular kind of diversity over time.

Other complications exist, as well. African Americans can be hard to identify even if scholarship panels are actively looking for them. Many applications do not include or are forbidden to include photos of applicants, and names do not necessarily offer a clue to ethnic or racial origin, resulting in a certain amount of guesswork. One scholarship committee thought they were increasing diversity by offering a scholarship to a student with an intellectual interest in rap and hip-hop only to discover that their African American scholar was a white southerner. Also at issue, some non-Americans focus on minorities, including those in their own country, only if they come from a deprived background. Years ago, one panel member of a prestigious European scholarship explained to me that she had cast her vote against a middle-class minority candidate because "he was not underprivileged." She had apparently not applied this means to test white candidates.

When encouraging an African American student to apply for a scholarship, keep in mind the question of expectations. When looking at minority candidates, international scholarships will want to see the usual criteria of academic excellence fulfilled. They will likely look for a connection to the African American community but not fret if one is not there. If it is clear the candidate is a minority, many scholarship providers want evidence of comfort with the wider world. Of course, they want to see proof of leadership, as well, and here, surprisingly, some excellent African Americans candidates may stumble.

Because of their difficult history in the United States, one in which people led despite not having an elected position, African American ideas about what constitutes leadership may not precisely match that of scholarship panels. African Americans tend to rank obvious leadership qualities and potential along with holding positions of leadership. Students in the African American community who are intelligent, hardworking, and active in clubs or community organizations as members will often see themselves as leaders along with their peers who have founded or run activities as officers.

Many prestigious scholarships tend, however, to interview students with CVs containing identifiable leadership roles. These perspectives are different enough that student needs to be alerted early on to seek leadership or standout positions. Ideally, they should seriously investigate clubs and activities at the college of their choice while they are still in high school, and when they are admitted, students must learn to speak up in class and develop a good relationship with professors in their core subject. Clearly, if a student has a job or volunteers in the community, panels will balance (or more likely prefer) this experience against officer positions in clubs.

Why wouldn't an exceptional student naturally do this? Experience and reactions to race situations are different for each individual. A student may feel too insecure in the new college environment to seek leadership positions that he failed to achieve in secondary school because he did not look the part. Her teachers in high school also may have been distant, seeing her as a black student rather than as a student.

Developing relationships with professors is crucial because a subject that can be pursued overseas is an excellent motivating factor for a student to study abroad, and for scholarships it of course is essential. A supportive professor can also assuage anxious family members that the experience will be useful in career terms.

Strategy Suggestions

To move forward, fellowship and study abroad officers should work together and consider adopting the following actions:

- Coordinate with the admissions officers so that students are aware of and knowledgeable about study abroad and its advantages even before they apply.
- Organize individual or small-group meetings for students with African American alums, scholar alums, or others who can speak from experience in a positive way about living abroad.
- Incorporate parent communications into student communications about study abroad benefits.
- Create bullet points emphasizing the practical value of the experience in terms of marketable skills.
- Contact African American alums who have worked abroad to get advice and anecdotes for the sales pitch.
- Never avoid the subject of racial fears—listen and learn from stated concerns.
- Ask embassies for a Q&A on race and society, including the situation of counterpart minorities, so that students have a firsthand perspective and meet interesting representatives, as well.
- Encourage overseas program directors to speak directly and personally to students about what to expect in their programs.

African American Organization Outreach

Finally, reach out to African American organizations. Many of them are at the forefront of encouraging international exposure for young people. They likely are already interested in and may themselves possess international connections and will happily support the mission of publicizing study abroad opportunities. Important organization contacts include churches, African American fraternities and sororities, and African American media. Publicizing in professional journals with African American memberships may be another way of reaching students and parents. Lack of knowledge about study abroad and the variety of programs offered is another documented issue for recruitment.

In summary, although there are some historical and contemporary barriers to attracting more African Americans to apply for scholarships and study abroad, a strategy involving like-minded colleagues and African American organizations and, especially, African American alumni has the potential to produce results. If the challenge of recruiting more African Americans were easy it, would have been solved long ago. Those who are taking on this agenda are doing important work, and it is appreciated by the many African Americans who have benefited and continue to benefit from their studies abroad.

7

Honoring the Code
The Ethics of Scholarship Advising

SUZANNE McCRAY

Suzanne McCray, vice provost for enrollment and associate professor of higher education at the University of Arkansas, has also directed the Office of Nationally Competitive Awards since establishing the program in 1998. Prior to assuming the position in enrollment, she was the associate dean of the Honors College. For three years she served on the national program review committee for the Coca-Cola Scholarship, and she currently is on the selection committee for the Morris Udall Scholarship. She has been an active member of NAFA since its founding, serving as its vice president from 2001 to 2003 and its president from 2003 to 2005. She has edited four volumes of the NAFA proceedings and was the cochair of the ethics committee that created the NAFA Code of Ethics. Prior to her work at the University of Arkansas, she served as a codirector of the Anglo-American Library at the University of Cluj-Napoca in Cluj, Romania.

Academic integrity is a value critically important to universities and colleges no matter their size, no matter whether they are public or private. Many have honor codes that they ask students to sign before enrolling in their first class.[1] Most have academic integrity policies that vary in levels of specificity and availability.[2] All have some sort of judiciary group to address infractions and to send the message that degrees from the institution have been honorably awarded to students who have completed their own work. Foundations expect the same. They have students certify that their work is their own. They also want to award their honors to those with integrity. Individual scholarship advisors, if they serve students well, also embrace academic integrity codes.[3] Ethics has been central to the National Association of Fellowships Advisors since its inception.

At Truman and Marshall Scholarships: Breaking the Code, a 1999 conference held in Arkansas, legendary advisor Nancy Twiss spoke about the importance of ethics. She stressed that it was essential for advisors to understand how to help students apply effectively but that they must be careful to advise students appropriately. She was right on the mark. Although advisors need to provide accurate information—breaking the code, from that perspective—advisors must also safeguard the process by ensuring students' applications always are, down to the last word, their own. Honoring that ethical code is essential as advisors work with talented, ambitious students.

In chapter 11 of this volume, Beth Powers details the development of NAFA, including its goals and purposes. One essential reason for the creation of the organization was to validate professional fellowship advising and, in doing so, to safeguard the process of assisting students as they apply for the world's most competitive scholarships.

In 2008 then-president Paula Warrick put together an ethics committee comprising ten people from foundations, private colleges, and public institutions charged with drafting a code of ethics. That group created a guide for dealing with the tough, often complex issues associated with students, advisors, faculty, institutions, and foundations, and that code was unanimously approved by the NAFA membership. The points discussed in this essay center on the application not the review or interview side of the process. What can and should a university expect of its students, its faculty, and its advisors, as well as its administration, throughout the application experience and the ensuing results? This is the main question the NAFA Code of Ethics addresses, and it is the focus of the following discussion.

Ethics and the Application Process

AN HONOR CODE FOR STUDENTS

Student cheating at universities across the country is problematic. According to recent studies, nearly two-thirds of all students say they have cheated at some time during their careers.[4] According to a *New York Times* article by Richard Perez-Pena, students cheat because it is easy and goes relatively unpunished. In it he interviews Donald McCabe, a well-known researcher on cheating patterns, who concludes that pressures and fierce competition have caused students "to excuse more from themselves and other students, and that's abetted by the adults around them." McCabe continues, "There have always been struggling students who cheat to survive, but more and more, there are students at the top who cheat to thrive."[5]

There is no more intensely pressured environment than national award competitions. Advisors may assume that their students would never cheat or that they could never cheat, since a personal statement cannot be plagiarized. In the fall of 2010, however, Adam Wheeler, a then senior at Harvard, had the audacity to do exactly that. He had been lying and cheating for years at and about various institutions, but he did not get caught until he submitted a Fulbright and a Rhodes application to his resident dean for endorsement.[6] The level of fraud in this student's career was stunning and unusual, even when considering national statistics on cheating in college. His résumé looked impressive, but it was based on dishonestly achieved gains. If Professor James Simpson had not recognized that the prose was nearly word for word from his colleague Stephen Greenblatt, Wheeler may have been shortlisted for the Rhodes.[7]

What happened at Harvard was, of course, unusual. Wheeler was guilty of misrepresenting himself long before he arrived there. Even while on probation, with the threat of prison to dissuade him, he sent out a fraudulent résumé for a nonpaying five-hour-per-week internship.[8] He is not the student we normally have to guard against, but his behavior did create a discussion on campuses about how to safeguard our admissions processes and how to make sure that students' résumés reflect work they have actually done.[9] Advisors probably do not need to be on the outlook for Adam Wheelers. Most advisors will work their entire lives and never meet such a person, but advisors should still remember the case, understand that it is possible that variations of his behavior could happen at any institution, and be on the outlook for exaggeration, for padding, and for misrepresentation should they occur. Many students accept spin as a part of doing business. Advisors need to ask questions of a student or of others if an application looks too good to be true.

The NAFA Code of Ethics makes clear that students "should ensure that all application materials, including but not limited to personal statements, résumés, proposals, essays, shall be the sole and original work of the applicant," citing paraphrased material and providing sources.[10] Students should also be encouraged to delete any activities in which they had no real substantive involvement. Exaggeration in this context is fraud, and of course, it is lying in any context.

This should come as no surprise to any senior, but a review of this expectation in general and individual meetings is prudent. If an advisor is suspicious but cannot locate a source, then using a product like Turnitin could help ease or confirm concerns. Plagiarism in an essay or other materials for any nationally competitive awards should be treated as it would be for a class assignment.[11]

FACULTY MENTORS

Faculty members who mentor and advise students can help reinforce values of academic honesty. Most do—insisting that students do their own work, requiring that they take credit only when credit is due and give credit where it is appropriate, and keeping letters of recommendation realistic and confidential. Faculty members sometimes do things, though, that encourage students to think shortcuts at times are acceptable.

Most advisors know of a faculty member who has asked a student to draft a letter of recommendation. Faculty members may contend that they will edit the letter and refuse to sign anything that is not true. No matter how it is couched, however, the student is drafting a letter that she is not supposed to see, and in some cases she may sign away the right to read a letter she has in essence created. This situation is unfair to the student in many ways. It is not only inappropriate but also awkward for someone to sing her own praises—at least that is the hope—and in trying to do so modestly, the student will likely generate prose that does not do her justice. These students also learn something indelible about the faculty member and their relationship. The NAFA Code of Ethics addresses this issue and states that this practice is unacceptable, and many offices hand out the code at faculty and student workshops, emphasizing that student-written letters are prohibited.[12]

When writing letters of recommendation, faculty members should include only the information that they can confirm and not simply repeat information from the student's résumé without checking if it is an accurate assessment of the student's abilities and commitments. This has the potential to be time consuming, but at the very least faculty should engage in a conversation with the student to determine what sort of commitment was really involved in the items on the list. Writing that a student is an active and dedicated volunteer for the Red Cross when the student gave blood once obviously is misleading and would not well serve the student in an interview when she is asked about her role. Indicating that a student is fluent in Arabic only to have him be discombobulated by questions asked in Arabic serves no one well. Letters that are accurate assessments of the applicant's abilities and achievements, as well as the student's potential for future success, are the most persuasive. If these realistic assessments also include high praise, then the institution has nominated the right candidate.

Not only can faculty mentors provide invaluable advice about the actual research, the readability of the essay, and student's presentation of the information, but they can also conduct an important check that the student has appropriately cited sources and given credit where appropriate. Such a review is essential and safeguards the process. Fellowships advisors cannot for the most part provide this oversight. Of course, many scholarships do not require institutional endorsement, but research mentors are expected to provide letters of recommendation. Institutions should encourage research mentors to review these applications as a part of a standard practice. This practice is not new for faculty. They regularly guide students through similar processes when students are in labs and when they are writing master's theses and doctoral dissertations.[13]

Publications can also be a question mark in a student's application. Many faculty members include students who are in their labs in publications even if the students have had very little direct input because they are part of the intellectual climate in the lab or because they have made a contribution in an indirect way. Pardis Sabeti, an assistant professor at Harvard who published as an undergraduate, supports inclusiveness because students "are always intellectually involved—not just a pair of hands in the lab."[14] This can be true of undergraduate as well as graduate students. Long lists of names are included in publications for a variety of reasons, and reasons for the inclusion of student names are similarly varied. Though a student may have completed the bulk of the work and in fact be the major contributor, the research fits within other work in the lab, and so additional names are included. A student may have completed less of the work but is working on a tangential but relevant project, and again, a student may have been part of the intellectual climate.

The order of the names does not always indicate the amount of work contributed to the project. In many fields the first name in the list signals the main contributor. In others it is the last, or the names can simply be listed in alphabetical order.[15] One lab has a complicated point system, and anyone with more than one hundred points on any given project is named in a resulting article.[16] These practices can even cause concerns about faculty vitas. Some tenure and promotion committees are now asking for the percentage of work done and no longer simply accept a list of publications as the full story of active scholarship. Like universities, major journals are working to get a handle on this and have "guidelines for authorship, but the protocols still haven't exactly stabilized, and they rarely address author order."[17] This complex issue cannot be resolved or even addressed by individual faculty or fellowships advisors, but students would do well to make clear their level of involvement in and contribution to a publication in an application for a competitive award or a graduate program.

Fellowships advisors can assist faculty members by holding meetings to discuss letters of recommendation and provide guidelines, including the NAFA Code of Ethics, to faculty and students, outlining the process for those rare occasions when a student does not live up to the institution's honor code or academic integrity policies. Inviting the provost, vice chancellor, or vice president for academic affairs is a good way to help faculty understand how much their role is valued, as well as their importance in maintaining the department's, the college's, and the institution's reputation.

ETHICS AND FELLOWSHIPS ADVISORS

The first NAFA conference, held in Tulsa, included a plenary session on ethics, and a similar session has been held at each subsequent conference. The Tulsa session's panel comprised two advisors (one a philosopher) and a college president. All of the attendees agreed that an ethical approach was critical. Advisors who act inappropriately and whose support invades the application process compromise themselves, their students, and their institutions. Andrew Brownstein, a reporter from the *Chronicle of Higher Education,* attended the conference. He too was interested in the ethical aspects of what advisors do. The opening line of the resulting article makes that clear: "Sophisticated programs bring awards to more colleges, thrilling presidents and donors, but are all the efforts ethical?"[18] In the article his answer clearly is no, not all. Brownstein provides an example of a faculty member in the Midwest who thought he had discovered a formula for winning and was willing to impose it on his students.

The majority of advisors knows that this approach is wrongheaded. No one wins in such circumstances. There is no formula. Advisors and foundations do not always know, however, the best response to every question or to all situations. At NAFA conferences, both regional and national, participants review a variety of challenging ethical situations that advisors and foundations have faced. Situations can be complex and solutions may vary, but advisors have established guidelines in the NAFA Code of Ethics to help them make good choices, even in previously uncharted waters.

The NAFA Code of Ethics makes clear that foundations, advisors, and institutions have responsibilities and ethical obligations to their various communities and to society as a whole. The code outlines the basics of what advisors should and should not do and what they must insist that applicants do and not do. It is intended as a guide, though, not as a law. No watchdog will punish advisors who violate the code. Advisors and faculty know, however, if something does not feel right, and the student, who has not necessarily read the code, knows when something crosses a line.

In *Beyond Winning: National Scholarship Competitions and the Student Experience,* Louis Blair writes an article titled "Having a Winner Every Time in the Truman Competition."[19] At first glance, the title is a little scary, sounding as if a formula for winning exists. Winning for Blair is not necessarily about being awarded a scholarship. For the student, winning is about learning, developing, and planning a future regardless of the scholarship at hand. For the advisor, winning needs to be about pointing students to the right scholarship or graduate program, ensuring students have access to the support materials that foundations and scholarship programs provide, and opening doors that will allow students to realize, in one way or another, the plans they are shaping and reshaping. In honoring this code, advisors help students win whether they receive a particular scholarship or not. Advisors win every time in such circumstances, as do their institutions.

Advisors who write sentences, paragraphs, or more of students' essays (if such do exist) greatly harm their profession, their institution, and most important, their students. At a plenary session of the 2011 conference in Chicago, Elliot Gerson, American secretary for the Rhodes Trust, remarked:

> Now the essay—I have to confess that, even though we have people sign documents that state, "This essay is my own work," frankly none of us believes that anymore. The sense is that most essays are edited and reedited dozens of times by twenty-odd people, even though I think usually the second draft is going to be a lot better than the hundredth draft. The essay is still important, but frankly I do not think it is as important as it used to be because we just do not believe it is the person's own work.[20]

This assessment is devastating and one that advisors need to understand is out there and work to remediate. Advisors do read essays. They provide advice, point out grammatical errors, and let students know if an essay lacks sufficient specific information about the plan of study or if a point being made misses the mark, but they do not write for the student. If they do, they are "shadow scholars" in the worst possible sense.[21]

Given that advisors should be cautious when engaging students about their writing, little debate exists on intervening at the level of grammar. If students are unclear about the rules of grammar, they should learn them and make the appropriate changes—unless they are hoping to make a strong point that is reinforced by grammatical innovation, though students need to understand the risks involved with this approach. Students have a voice, and that voice has an appeal. That voice also will be the one present during their interviews. Recommending that students edit themselves out is not good advice. The second edit may indeed be the best.

Suggesting the essay formulas Brownstein mentions is unwise, and they may deaden a student's voice. English teachers in secondary schools often encourage essay plans or rubrics that tell students how to draft a first paragraph, where to place the thesis statement, how to connect paragraphs, what coordinating conjunctions to use, and more. Many of us learned to write using a three-point enumeration essay as a model. Teachers have a good reason for liking such methods. Essays-by-the numbers can help students who write poorly write more effectively. Though they can help D and C students write B papers, essays-by-design can sap the life from powerful prose and quickly reduce the quality and the vitality of A-level writers' work. Students who reveal an authentic spark are more likely to be interviewed and more likely to be successful in an interview.

An advisor should provide guidance and then get out of the student's way, encouraging the student to develop a voice that persuasively conveys engagement and vision. Students will likely edit applications extensively several times before submitting, just as they would a major paper. And proofreading is key and can be often mistaken for editing. A student should proofread carefully several times after the last edit is completed. Helping students create a healthy habit of repeatedly proofreading their work is an important part of the job that will have a long-term value to the student.

Of course, aspirations, ideas, prose, and content should always be the student's. If the process is to be meaningful and helpful beyond winning an award, then it must have educational value in the way that advice given to students writing a thesis or a dissertation has educational value that goes beyond the individual exercise. If it does not, then other ethical questions must be addressed about the time, effort, and funds that institutions (in all of their various forms, whether private or public, Ivy League or land grant, four-year or two-year, large, medium, or small) across the country invest in students who are applying. Blair is right that the application process is a way for advisors to assist students in winning every time they apply, regardless of the outcome for a given award. In chapter 8 of this volume, Betsy Vardaman provides a list of learning outcomes often experienced, in various combinations, by fellowship applicants. Improving writing skills heads the list. Richard Light surveyed more than 1,600 students at Harvard and reports in *Making the Most of College* that he was surprised when the survey revealed a strong student attachment to improving writing skills: "I would have guessed that they value good writing, but I didn't realize how deeply many of them care about it, or how strongly they hunger for specific suggestions about how to improve it."[22] Advising students on how to write more effectively is a valid part of the job if the advisor is trained.

An advisor can provide advice on an approach to effective writing without changing who the student is, affecting the student's writing style, or changing in any way the student's long-term goals. In the same way, a coach can give advice on the arc of a shot or hold practices to help players relax and give them confidence, but the coach cannot turn players into shooters, no matter the number of practices or the number of conversations. The player is the shooter and stands alone with the ball in her hands.

An additional challenge for advisors concerns endorsement letters. Advisors often draft letters for provosts or chancellors who are asked to endorse students they may or may not know well. Advising offices in collaboration with the nominating or endorsing office in question must make decisions about whether this is acceptable. Many advisors feel that it is not and instead provide information to the foundations about how the letter is to be written. In some offices the provost, chancellor, or president cosigns the letter with the advisor or with the chair of the nomination committee to indicate the process. Other offices are comfortable drafting such a letter because the person signing may feel like this approach provides a fairer description of the student's accomplishments and the trust level is such to warrant it.

On a NAFA-sponsored trip to the United Kingdom, this issue was hotly debated among the participants. Jonathan Taylor, then head of the Marshall Aid Commission, agreed that drafting the endorsement letters for busy presidents and provosts was acceptable as long as the institution was clearly willing to endorse the candidate and the upper administration had faith in those drafting the letter. In both student-drafted recommendations and advisor-drafted endorsements, drafting letters is involved, but the right answer may not be as clear in both instances. The NAFA code addresses one explicitly, but not the other. The line for endorsement letters is tougher to draw. At the very least, an institution should be thoughtful, collaborative, and reflective about its process for endorsing candidates.

Ethics and Institutions

Universities and colleges want their students to be successful in their endeavors both during and after the college experience. Evaluating the path to this success can be difficult. It has certainly proven challenging in assessing faculty success. One of the reasons that scholarship has become a major part of faculty job descriptions is that it can be evaluated. Articles, books, and presentations can be counted. Activity can be quantified. Success in the classroom is less easy to assess; it seems less objective.

By pointing to where students pursue postgraduate study, providing statistics on job placement, and celebrating students who win nationally competitive awards, institutions provide tangible proof that they are preparing students well for the future. This dependence on visible student outcomes can give rise to institutional pressure on offices that advise these students. If an institution does not look at the overall value of the program and narrowly focuses on which institutions win what and how often, an unhealthy culture can arise. Institutions that develop quotas for particular scholarships, insisting that an office produces so many of this or that scholar in a given number of years, lose sight of what such offices are about and may not have a realistic understanding of the number of exceptional students across the country who apply. Institutions would do well to consider Kant's imperative in the *Critique of Practical Reason*: "So act as to treat humanity whether in thine own person or in that of any other, in every case as an end withal, never as means only."[23] For universities promoting national competitions, that translates as *think about and work toward what is best for the student as an end in itself not as a necessary step to a prize.*

The NAFA code of ethics highlights institutions' responsibilities to "emphasize, through publicity and infrastructure, the value of students' intellectual and personal development through the fellowship process" and, "when evaluating scholarship programs, use techniques that attempt to measure the value of the process of applying for fellowships, and take into account the highly competitive nature of fellowship competitions."[24] The code also points to core values that all advisors have agreed upon: integrity, collaboration, respect, and fairness. If we situate the issues that trouble us in this context, then we will arrive at solutions that we can feel good about and defend.

8

Recalculating
A Sojourn down Scholarship Road to the Deep Heart's Core

ELIZABETH VARDAMAN

Elizabeth Vardaman is an associate dean in the College of Arts and Sciences at Baylor University in Waco, Texas. An exchange professor in China and assistant director for several Baylor abroad programs in England and the Netherlands, she has extensively traveled on behalf of the university and led the first NAFA tour of British higher education. Her overview of that trip, "Keys to the United Kingdom," is published in Beyond Winning: National Scholarship Competitions and the Student Experience. *She also authored "Coin of the Realm: Graduate Education in Britain," published in* Nationally Competitive Scholarships: Serving Students and the Public Good. *She has served as a scholarship advisor since 1998 and was a charter member of NAFA. She and Jane Morris (Villanova University) cochaired the 2006 NAFA Higher Education Symposia in the United Kingdom and the Republic of Ireland.*

The creation of the National Association of Fellowships Advisors happily coincided with my university's decision to provide institutional support to students bidding for nationally competitive scholarships. My memories of the first ten years include some heady days filled with energy and bright promise. The road map to our destination—a vibrant scholarship program—was clear: we informed our students of the array of astonishing foundations and opportunities, set out timelines, tailored workshops, built websites, fine-tuned our recruitment process, and tweaked the system for vetting recommendation letters. We gleaned rich insights shared at NAFA conferences and jubilated when our students brought home the gold. Nevertheless, as the years went by, the more I learned the craft of our profession, the more I found myself equating having a vibrant program with winning.

The past several winters, however, my life's GPS has been suggesting some recalculating might be in order. One particular day is etched in my mind. I had just parked in front of a Starbucks on a crisp, cold afternoon. Nervous, weary, exuberant with hope, my heart was running the gamut of emotions. A wonderful candidate who had interviewed for one of those prized fellowships that go only to the lucky few would soon hear the results. Then my mobile phone buzzed a text message alert. "This can't be good," I reasoned. "He would surely want to shout out his news if he has won." I did not want to risk what reality might have in store, so I put the phone away, went inside, and ordered a chai latte. All things were still possible. Visions of celebration and student success danced in my head, and the bells in my mind pealed with the new respect and support our office would garner. (The dream was short, but the dream was happy.)

As any advisor might guess, he did not win. The odds are always stacked against the individual student, but that does not diminish a student's pain at the setback. This student's pain was real, and I was both discouraged and filled with self-doubt. My first impulse was to wonder whether I had missed my calling; surely, running a tea shop might have been a better fit for my skills. Yet a deeper reality eventually brought me back to my senses. All advisors experience the disappointment of having incredibly talented, dedicated students not win a scholarship that would set them on a path for realizing important academic and service goals. Win or not, something compelling remains, though, about this profession. Otherwise, no one would participate in or subject candidates to the grueling competition against such odds year after year. In truth, when I raised myself up from self-scrutiny, I found a less egocentric and, one would hope, more profitable line of inquiry to pursue: what formidable roadblocks and detours had been imposed over the past decade on Scholarship Road that might have caused me and perhaps other advisors to veer off course?

If we measure our value by our universities' successes, then many scholarship advisors and their supervisors are surely reassessing their reasons for this journey and seeking clarity about their destinations. The facts are sobering. Budget cuts have eliminated some amazing scholarships. Other high-profile foundations have had to reduce the number of fellowships they offer. More universities and, thus, more applications have entered the fray. Resources within universities have tightened. More high-achieving postgraduate and graduate students are competing for awards in a tough economy. Additionally, NAFA's ongoing engagement with hundreds of representatives has undoubtedly raised the level of excellence in the application pool nationwide.

Given these realities, whether individual students always garner national acclaim or not, scholarship programs must affirm critically important values to academic institutions, to best practices in higher education, and to the realization of the foundations' ideals. Many principles—or signposts, to push the metaphor—attest to the unique benefits scholarship advising offices are designed to achieve. These principles help us correct our course if we become sidetracked or need to recalculate our journey or the ends toward which we are speeding.

Awakening Students to the Link between Liberal Learning and Life

Dr. Andrew Delbanco and many other academic leaders remind us that a college education should be, first and foremost, "an aid to reflection, a place and process whereby young people take stock of their talents and passions and begin to sort out their lives in a way that is true to themselves and responsible to others." Amid a culture overwhelmed with gadgets and cyber faces, Delbanco asserts that college should show students "how to think and how to choose."[1]

Scholarship offices are one of the places within universities wherein faculty and staff endeavor to help students do exactly that—learn to think and to choose. Scholarship advisors reach some of the university's best and brightest and build bridges from students' questions regarding what is worth living for to skills and professional goals that resonate with their values and their deep heart's core. All of us have encountered hugely talented undergraduates who have not dealt with larger life questions through their regular classroom experiences but who ponder such questions through their interactions with our offices and thought-provoking essay questions designed by foundations keen to motivate such inquiry. These functions and these offices serve as models to reaffirm the ultimate aims of a liberal education.

Certainly, some, maybe even many, students do not receive that larger life lesson in college. Lincoln Steffens's *Autobiography*, read during my own college sojourn, remains relevant to our enterprise as well. His reminiscences of life as an undergraduate, albeit in late nineteenth-century America, include this biting assessment:

> *No one ever developed for me the relation of any of my required subjects to those that attracted me; no one brought out for me the relation of anything I was studying to anything else, except, of course, to that wretched degree. Knowledge was absolute, not relative, and it was stored in compartments, categorical and independent. The relation of knowledge to life, even to student life, was ignored, and as for questions, the professors asked them not the students, and the students, not the teachers, answered them—in examinations.*[2]

Leaping forward one-hundred-plus years, Richard Light's important book *Making the Most of College* is based on interviews with 1,600 students at Harvard (Light interviewed 400 of the undergraduates himself) in his search to understand students' views on how to break down the compartments and connect knowledge acquired to life experienced on a college campus and beyond. In order to learn about effective advising experiences, he spoke with thirty Rhodes and Marshall Scholars, twenty-two of whom told Light that "at key points in their college years an academic advisor asked questions, or posed a challenge, that forced them to think about the relationship of their academic work to their personal lives."[3] Light also records one Rhodes Scholar's life-changing reflection on the interaction with his advisor: "In retrospect, my advisor's pushing me to relate my work at college to my personal concerns is what encouraged me to do philosophy while preparing for medical school. I am sure I will be a better doctor because of this good advice. And I think I can be a better son, too."[4] Such insight and the affirmation of such intense mentoring are defining aspects of the application experience and have been significant parts of the role of scholarship advisors and of NAFA from the inception of the organization.

Additionally, advising services are no longer exclusively reserved for the well born or the financially secure. The transformation of universities from havens for the elite in the early twentieth century to inclusive institutions now has broad parallels within our profession. The cultural shift that took place in colleges when the G.I. Bill opened the doors gave way to the baby boomers. More access for women in the 1960s and the 1970s was followed by the racial, ethnic, and economically based diversification of the past three decades, including the increase in international students. All of these expansions of access have met with the affirmation of diverse, talented, visionary applicant pools across all groups. Every advisor has been affected by memorable encounters with a first-generation college student who studied in the car at night in high school when the family had no money to pay for electricity or a new American who worked three jobs on the side to pay her tuition because she would become an artist or die. These "hungry hearts" often tell their stories to scholarship advisors when they tell no one else.[5] And scholarship foundations often want to meet these striving, passionate applicants who have overcome adversity to attend college, to aim for greatness.

There also are many "midway people" (Lionel Trilling's term) for whom the scholarship process becomes integral to the purpose of college, as well. Our offices become the crucible "where young people fight out among and within themselves contending ideas of the meaningful life and where they discover that self-interest need not be at odds with concern for one another."[6] We all have faces etched in our memories that wrestled with the question, "What is it that is worth wanting?"[7] Isn't that question the still-point of the process advisors are engaged in as they encourage students to take stock of their talents and interests and sort out a life that is not only true to themselves but also responsible to others?

Foundations often articulate their commitments to social concerns, to ambassadorship, to academic excellence, and to citizenship in their mission statements. In presenting themselves to these foundations, students are encouraged to show how they are in the process of becoming critics of and conscientious spokespersons for society. As a result, they may be motivated to take on leadership roles that address serious problems facing communities at home and abroad. In other words, this process moves students far beyond becoming "world class hoop jumpers" to standing up for what they believe.[8] David Brooks argues that this kind of courage is "the central business of adulthood." He advocates for "finding serious things to tie yourself down to. The successful young adult is beginning to make sacred commitments—to a spouse, a community and calling—yet mostly hears about freedom and autonomy."[9] Competitive applicants for fellowships must both come to terms with their true passions and tie themselves to issues larger than themselves. This takes fortitude and moral courage.

In this way, scholarship offices synchronize steps with those who call for citizenship and democratic values to be advanced through higher education. Dr. Carol Schneider, president of the Association of American Colleges and Universities (AAC&U), reminds governors and all educators that "education's first duty is to democracy."[10] Derek Bok underscores a similar call to arms by noting that "faculties currently display scant interest in preparing undergraduates to be democratic citizens, a task once regarded as the principal purpose of a liberal education."[11] Those students who become models of good citizenship are "possessed of a democratic spirit marked by independent judgment, the freedom to measure action and to express disagreement, and the crucial responsibility never to tolerate tyranny."[12] More plainly put, part of the challenge students must confront, as Delbanco notes, is discerning "the difference between demagoguery and responsible arguments."[13] Thus, students must come "to detect when [someone] is talking rot."[14] Delbanco continues, asserting that this skill may be "the most important thing one can acquire in college."[15] All of this is to say that public intellectuals and leaders in higher education—including scholarship foundations and advisors—are keen to identify and support the courageous best and brightest who detect "rot" and stand up for what they believe, first finding themselves through service and then losing themselves into commitment to a heterogeneous civil society and its ideals.

Engaged Learning inside and outside the Classroom

The microcosm of a functioning democratic society is lived out in colleges across the United States. Scholarship offices help shape campus cultures as staff members encourage students to push past their comfort zones and into engaged learning environments both inside and beyond their academic responsibilities.

The image of a double helix signifies the unique and vital contributions that scholarship programs can make to students and to our larger enterprise as universities—even though the article that set my mind to this idea did not mention national scholarship programs or their efforts to enrich liberal learning outcomes.[16] Applauding a total learning experience that would intentionally weave together the formal classroom and life's larger laboratory, the essay urges leaders in student life to collaborate and plan ways for students' experiential learning to complement academic life. The resulting intertwine of academic courses purposefully in sync with service learning becomes a double helix (see Figure 1). This beautiful and inspiring graphic shows how advisors can help students incrementally invest themselves in a more complex and advanced weaving of both strands throughout college and how students can link their classroom experiences to campus, community, state, federal, and international entities in infinite varieties of ways—all to good effect for them and for society.

Advisors know the argument well. In fact, scholarship offices embody the double helix concept in every conversation we have with students interested in maximizing their college experience and bidding for national and international awards. So why did the scholarship advising field not make the experiential learning cut in Haefner and Ford's graphic ideal? Advising on nationally competitive awards is not limited to one strand of the double helix. Scholarship offices, when all the stars align, work both sides of the academic street, and our enterprise contributes to student learning outcomes within the classroom and far beyond. Some of those outcomes were enthusiastically enumerated at the 2011 NAFA conference in Chicago when Cindy Schaarschmidt (Drexel), Beth Fiori (Cornell), and Kate Dailinger (Yale) led a session entitled "It's Not Just about Winning: Learning Outcomes for Fellowship Applicants, How to Assess and Communicate Them." The list that NAFA members provided to that presentation is long and instructive (see Figure 2).[17] Thus, our work is validated through the progression of academic and engaged learning strands as they intertwine from first year to graduation for each applicant we mentor. No wonder there is a high burnout rate for professionals in the advising field.

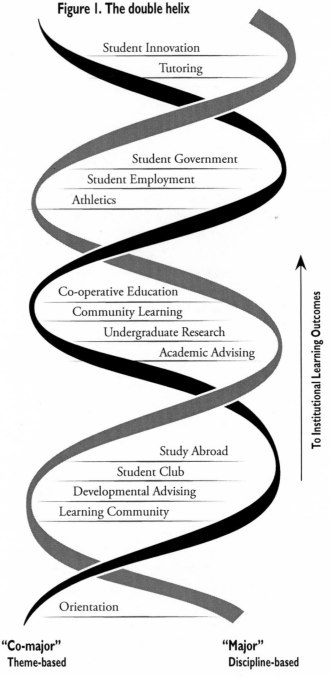

Figure I. The double helix

Student Innovation

Tutoring

Student Government

Student Employment

Athletics

Co-operative Education

Community Learning

Undergraduate Research

Academic Advising

Study Abroad

Student Club

Developmental Advising

Learning Community

Orientation

To Institutional Learning Outcomes

"Co-major"
Theme-based

"Major"
Discipline-based

Source: Jeremy Haefner and Deborah L. Ford, "The Double Helix: A Purposeful Pathway to an Intentional and Transformational Liberal Education," *Liberal Education* 96, no. 2 (Spring 2010): 52. Reprinted with permission from *Liberal Education*. Copyright held by the Association of American Colleges and Universities.

Figure 2. Learning Outcomes List, NAFA Conference, Chicago 2011

Learning Outcomes

In the process of applying for fellowships, students

- improve their writing (clear, concise, pointed, persuasive);
- hone their interview skills;
- practice networking (cultivating relationships with professors, etc.);
- attain time-management skills;
- communicate their research and goals to a larger audience;
- learn how to follow directions;
- start thinking about graduate school;
- formulate a clearer sense of values;
- find the best path to fulfilling *their* potential as *they* see it (not their parents);
- develop self-awareness and a sense of purpose;
- become independent thinkers;
- identify strengths and weaknesses (with the hope to improve the latter);
- clarify how they can make useful and meaningful contributions to the world;
- find out that trying hard is more important than winning;
- learn how to meet rigorous expectations and open themselves up to critique in order to do so;
- realize the importance of diversifying their college experience (high grades do not suffice);
- discover that many things in life are completely out of their control;
- learn how to cope with disappointment.

How to Assess Learning Outcomes

- student (video) interviews
- portfolios of writing samples
- student surveys
- reflective writing exercises
- inviting this year's applicants to talk to prospective candidates

For further discussion, see Meg Franklin, "Assessment of Fellowship Programs," *NAFA Journal,* Summer 2007, http://www.nafadvisors.org/journal_2007/assessment.htm.

Indeed, the multidimensional aspirations, expectations, and require-ments for national scholarship offices explain the plethora of places within organizational charts where such offices are located. They answer not only to academic schools and honors colleges but also to provost's offices, to career services, to admissions offices, to centers for social commitment, to undergraduate research, to financial aid offices, to international program centers, to student life, and to centers for undergraduate engagement—to name a few.

It is tempting to make much of this information—perhaps, suggesting that the work of a national scholarship office gives vitality to and complements the objectives of all of these divisions of our schools. Nevertheless, no matter the variety of units within which this work is performed, the office ultimately is bound to and identifies with learning outcomes enumerated in college mission statements and in Liberal Education and America's Promise (LEAP) objectives within AAC&U. Scholarship applicants develop intellectual and practical skills such as critical thinking, complex reasoning, writing, and speaking.[18]

Though critics, such as the authors of *Academically Adrift,* lament undergraduates' lack of growth in academic skills over their four years in college, they also encourage universities to "promote organizational cultures emphasizing student academic engagement, not just social engagement and student retention."[19] Though not directly referenced in these texts, the scholarship advisor's work is affirmed by the call to shore up and intensify the academic efforts in higher education because this special group of advisors understands the importance of both academic and social engagement, appreciating and fostering many other educational outcomes not always documented in quantitative assessments.

Conversation, Concentration, Failure, and an Ounce of Wisdom

Long ago Jacques Barzun, then dean of faculties at Columbia University, posited some intangibles that college students have the right to insist upon experiencing and may then hold dear ever after. One of those rights is to participate in and savor the art of a meaningful conversation, the kind of candid give and take that suspends time, making people lean forward in their chairs. With advisors, students are safe to spout out convictions and then contradict what they just said. Advisors are not giving them a grade that shows up on a transcript. Additionally, in a world of sometimes snarky electronic distractions and virtual chat rooms, these authentic confrontations provide space to breathe and think. A kind of deep-down freshness may be produced that many undergraduates have rarely known.

And what happens in our offices does not always stay in our offices. Instead, conversations that begin here proliferate, go viral, and enrich discussions with faculty mentors and beyond. One of the vital factors that foundations wish could be discerned from applicants' documents (but cannot) answers the questions, "Who are your friends and what do you talk about when you are together?"[20] As dynamic and essential as the Internet and social media have become to our culture, face-to-face exploration of issues of substance—"lateral learning"—encourages students to realize how much they can learn from one another.[21]

Bidding for these awards also requires students to chisel out time to give themselves fully to the enterprise. To write well, they will be put to the test and must block out the sirens that call to them from smart phones, computers, the Internet, YouTube, televisions, and Twitter. The very qualities that have enabled them to excel in myriad fields may now become a barrier to success. Thus, these often overextended high achievers must narrow the spectrum of experiences upon which they expend themselves, sidelining some, eliminating others entirely. Multitasking does not always work. Applicants understand they will have to gather themselves together into one place and focus. They may also have to meet and work with a librarian, which they will discover is a very positive experience. These seekers will remember the intensity of the mental and the emotional effort they had to expend to create these singular, strong essays.[22]

No one can predict the number of hours involved in producing a compelling essay that reveals something essential about the candidate, because "it takes as long as it takes."[23] Much like the creation of jazz compositions, the more times students circle around the basic melody of themselves, the more likely they are to emerge with essays that achieve the difficult balance between improvisation and structure, thus becoming unique and inimitable. From the intensity of this experience, there may emanate a kind of pride and inexpressible joy that distinguishes the work. For some, these essays are capstones for their college experience, their proudest achievements, the proof that concentration and passion for a job well done can be a glorious thing.

Some will indeed receive the tangible reward for having closed the door, turned off music, read deeply, striven for a new level of excellence, invested themselves in the hard work of writing careful, thoughtful prose, and determined to be not just good but great. The obvious reward? They may win. Everyone knows how sweet that is. But if they do not, these documents nevertheless distinguish the applicants and, as action plans, provide a sound basis on which to move forward. They may, like advisors, have to do some recalculation, but there is no question that many competitive applications for graduate and professional school, as well as Teach for America, Peace Corps, and other next steps, find their seedbeds in scholarship application essays. Additionally, at the end of the day many applicants are more self-aware, more certain of their pathways, and more confident they know what gives their lives meaning. The students have mined their depths through this process, come to realize their talents and goals, and determined to put them to service in the world.

Have these life lessons also enabled the applicants to grow a little wiser as they reflect in a dark mirror on whether the game is worth the candle? Many of our success-oriented students have never failed before. Those accomplished worthy many who inevitably must face that they came up short in the final tally of fortunate few confront themselves at this point. They can kill the messenger, berate the panels, and leave angry or bitter. Perhaps, though, they will learn that the processes are messy and imperfect, that there were ways in which they might have prevailed if only. . . . Value may be found, however, in calming down and recalculating. Drew Gilpin Faust, president of Harvard, recommends all freshmen read Kathryn Schulz's book *Being Wrong,* which "advocates doubt as a skill and praises error as the foundation of wisdom."[24] Such a book— and the sobering realities that face our students when the interview knocked them off their pins or some other error in the process doomed their bid for the award—may be just what is needed. Scholarship mentors walk beside those who risked and came up short; they are witnesses to the story, the disappointment, and ultimately the insight that almost always appears weeks or months later.

We watch and cheer for these students as they manage their successes and shortfalls. They become, in many cases, our heroes and "catch the heart off-guard and blow it open."[25] Because they are amazing, we are drawn like moths to the flame, back each year through them to begin again. I look at the photographs of students who have graced my world during these twelve NAFA years—some who grasped the brass ring and some who did not. (I recently danced at the wedding of my Starbucks scholar. He began a terrific PhD fellowship in the United States this past fall.) They give me hope for the future—all of them making a difference somewhere, somehow—fighting injustice, creating beauty, seeking truth, mending lives, and working hard to bring light to dark places. They have made me better than I meant to be, and the process of applying for scholarships made them better, too. More than that, our institutions are renewed by the sagas, hard knocks, hard work, grit, and resulting narratives engendered by these students and the unique road they travel through our offices.

Taking stock of the professional journey reminds advisors that we are engaged in a serious and serendipitous enterprise and that reflection and recalculation can yield renewal. (Learning that more scholarships are coming online, including the Rotary Foundation Global Grants, also elevates our anticipation of the coming scholarship seasons.) Whether the number of scholarship winners at our universities ebbs or flows in any given year, we have many reasons to take heart, to be renewed by the values and processes involved in our profession, and to not cease from the exploration we are engaged in—for the students and for our institutions. As T. S. Eliot reminds us in *Four Quartets,* using inspirational phrases such as "the drawing of this Love" and "the voice of this Calling," "The end of all our exploring / Will be to arrive where we started / And know the place for the first time." May it ever be so.

9

Coping with Common Challenges
Strategies for Success in Fellowship Advising

DANA KUCHEM, BETH POWERS, AND SUSAN WHITBOURNE

Dana Kuchem heads the Undergraduate Fellowship Office at The Ohio State University, where she has worked since obtaining her master's in higher education in 2005. She currently is a NAFA board member and member of the professional development and best practices, consultation, and assessment committees. A NAFA participant since 2005, she serves on the planning committee for the Atlanta 2013 conference, chairing the workshop for new advisors. As a fellowships advisor, she is most proud of receiving a Fulbright grant to Germany as part of the International Education Administrators program in 2011.

Beth Powers is the founder and director of the Office of Special Scholarship Programs at the University of Illinois–Chicago, where she has worked since 2000. Previously, she worked in fellowship and prelaw advising at Kansas

State University for four years. For NAFA she has served as a conference organizer, a member of the ethics committee, a board member, and vice president. She was president from 2005 to 2007 and is a founding member.

Susan Whitbourne *received her PhD in developmental psychology from Columbia University. A professor of psychology at the University of Massachusetts–Amherst since 1999, she directs the Office of National Scholarship Advisement. She is the author of over 140 refereed articles and book chapters and sixteen books (many in multiple editions and translations), including* The Search for Fulfillment *and the recently published* Handbook of Adult Development and Aging. *She writes the popular* Psychology Today *blog* Fulfillment at Any Age. *The recipient of a 2011 Presidential Citation from the American Psychological Association, she is the winner of national and campus teaching and advising awards. She has served in executive board and advisory roles for a variety of regional and national professional organizations. A member of NAFA since 1999, she currently is a board member who chairs the professional development committee, and she organized the 2012 study tour of Washington, DC.*

Fellowships advisors experience numerous personal challenges due to the unique features of the occupation. Advisors encourage students to participate in highly visible national competitions that are demanding on the emotional resources of these students. Many advisors are the sole operators of scholarship advising offices and have few colleagues on campus who understand the unusual nature of their positions. In addition, the stakes in such work are high. Upper-level college administrators, in addition to students, their families, and faculty, place high expectations on the outcomes of scholarship competitions, over which advisors have little control. Once advisors have connected students to the right scholarships, advised them on references, passed on the foundations' good advice, and offered their own accumulated wisdom, there is little more to do than wait for the outcome. In many cases these outcomes can take weeks or months to learn, and if the results do not meet the expectations of the students, the advisor, or the institution, the advisors must wait at least another year before starting the process again.

In the face of these challenges, how can advisors successfully manage the stresses of fellowship advising? To help answer this question, we present six prototypical scenarios that highlight some of the most-demanding challenges that advisors can face. After each, we provide concrete examples of strategies that the advisor can use to manage the stresses associated with the particular situation. At the end we present a set of common coping strategies that advisors can use to manage the stress of these and the more general situations that confront all of us at some point in our advising lives.

Scenario I

Erin directs the fellowship office at a midsized university that is very strong in the STEM fields. Her school has historically done very well in the Goldwater competition, producing two to three winners annually. They again have another competitive group of students applying for the four university nominations this year. Erin has been working with Bob, a geology student, for over two years. Bob has a very impressive résumé, having started research in high school. He has completed three different research experiences, been published, and presented at a professional conference. In addition, he holds a 3.98 GPA. Erin finds Bob to be the top candidate in the university's applicant pool this year. When the selection committee convenes, however, one of the very vocal committee members dismisses Bob off the bat, stating that geology is not viewed as a real science. Erin is torn, as she believes Bob is a very competitive candidate. She not only wonders if her vision is clouded because she knows the student so well but also is frustrated by the bias the committee member has demonstrated. She does not agree with the direction of the committee's nomination decisions and is wondering what, if anything, she should do.

POSSIBLE STRATEGIES

If possible, Erin can obtain concrete information from foundation representatives and faculty familiar with the selection process and find out why she and the faculty member have different views of the student and the type of research he wants to do. She can also consult the NAFA listserv to find out if her evaluation of the student is off base.

Erin could evaluate her own biases and see where they are coming from. Does she identify with the student, positively or negatively? Is there something about the faculty member that is causing her to react negatively to this person's suggestion?

Scenario 2

Tyler works as a fellowships advisor at a large public institution. His school has been a rather late entry into the fellowship world, but they have seen success with many awards, including the Truman, the Udall, the Goldwater, and the Fulbright, for each they have had at least one winner or finalist every year. This success leaves him confident that they have competitive students who are submitting competitive applications. For the past five years, however, he has been unable to make any headway with certain scholarships. He has read the profiles of previous winners, sat in on conference sessions given by the foundations themselves, and carefully studied the selection criteria. Tyler believes the students his institution sends forward should be competitive, but they have simply had no success. In addition, some of these foundations state that they do not provide feedback to applicants. He feels he is spinning his wheels and does not know how to gain more traction with these particular award programs.

POSSIBLE STRATEGIES

Tyler is doing the right things as an advisor, though he can keep trying to receive feedback from foundations. Even if this feedback is not specific to the particular student, Tyler can still benefit from learning about fields of study, appropriate responses, GPA issues, and other topics that could provide general information to help in advising future applicants.

Tyler should continue to put forward good candidates, but he also should consider shifting his priorities to scholarships for which he feels his students might have greater success and speaking to his supervisor about this new strategy.

Scenario 3

Frank directs the prestigious national scholarship office at a respectable but not top public university in California, where there is heavy competition from the top public and several private institutions. Although the university had several students win major scholarships, including one Rhodes, he has endured a dry spell for the past five years. His most competitive students either have not made the finalist stage or have made it to the finalist stage but not progressed beyond it. At the end of the scholarship season last year, he was feeling demoralized about the situation. He had difficultly coping with his disappointment and, therefore, offering encouragement to his student advisees. He is trying to find ways to overcome these feelings and be a better resource for his graduating seniors as they pursue applications for graduate school and future jobs. He also is feeling that despite his efforts, his school simply will not be able to produce the type of students who can win scholarships in this increasingly competitive environment.

POSSIBLE STRATEGIES

Instead of focusing only on the scholarships, Frank should collect data about his students' successes in other realms. He could conduct a survey of the students he has worked with over the years to determine where they are, possibly asking them to provide answers to open-ended questions in which they talk about how the scholarship application process helped them.

Frank should not define his identity as a professional on the basis of the results of each year's competitions. It is particularly important for him to focus on the process and not the results so that he does not impose his feelings onto his students. It would help Frank to remind himself that his students are benefiting from the scholarship application process.

Scenario 4

Barb is the director of her college's honors program. She feels constant pressure from upper-level administrators, including the college president, to produce winners. Although she has tried many times to explain to her higher-ups that winning is not everything, she feels that she is not making inroads in helping them to see the importance of the process of scholarship applications. She has plenty of evidence to show that her students have been successful after graduation in securing fellowship offers in doctoral programs, acceptance to top medical and law schools, and jobs in competitive fields. The president's office has made it clear, however, that it wants more-impressive data on scholarship applicants to justify continued support of scholarship advising.

POSSIBLE STRATEGIES

It is understandable that Barb is feeling stressed by the pressure of the higher administration. To counter this pressure, she should consider alternate means of assessment of the outcome of her advising. She can also conduct a microanalysis to determine which factors are predictive of scholarship success and encourage her administration to invest in these types of programs. This analysis could also include comparisons with peer institutions to see if the programs they are running would be feasible at her school.

Barb should be sure that she keeps careful statistics on the number of students she advises so that she can show how many she is working with over the course of the year. She can use these statistics to show that she is having an impact on students and contributing to happier alumni, a fact that can be a different type of point of pride for the administration.

Barb should also seek out scholarship opportunities that may be more attainable for her students.

Scenario 5

Corinne is an associate dean at a university that like many in the country has seen declining budgets and a decreasing ability to fill the jobs of departing employees. She has traditionally worked with the British and the Fulbright scholarships and has had success with students in these competitions, but due to the departure of a key staff member in the dean's office, she is now being asked to advise students on the Truman, the Udall, the Goldwater, the National Science Foundation, and all other awards not handled by the study abroad office. She has other college-related responsibilities that take up 50 percent of her time, and the college is unlikely to remove these responsibilities. Corinne wonders how she can avoid burn-out and maintain or improve scholarship results.

POSSIBLE STRATEGIES

Corinne can consider other strategies to expand her resources, including hiring a graduate assistant and using a staff person assigned to other duties to assist during crunch times. She also can more heavily rely on her committees, asking specific faculty members to mentor students for particular scholarships.

Corinne's job evaluation should be based on a fair set of metrics that take into account the staff resources available to her when compared with those resources available to other programs.

Scenario 6

Marcus was hired as a scholarship and health careers advisor at an urban university whose students are 35 percent first-generation college-going students and 40 percent first-generation immigrants. The university has a 65 percent six-year graduation rate. Many of the first-generation students graduated from the resource-challenged city school district, and although they were strong high school students, they struggle in college. Certain programs, such as a combined bachelor's and master's program in the social sciences, draw very talented students, as does the university's exceptional nursing program. The university's honors program is in its fifth year and is still developing programming. An alumnus who was pursuing a master's degree at the top-ranked state university recently won a Marshall Scholarship, and the president has invited Marcus to her office to discuss his plan to produce more of such scholars and to do so while they are still at the university. Marcus feels that most students at the school are not likely to be a good fit for the British scholarships and that this one was a rare exception, but he is not sure how to address this issue with the president.

POSSIBLE STRATEGIES

Marcus can use this encounter with the president to ask for more resources for the scholarship advising office. Drawing the attention of the president to this success could be an important step toward expanding the scholarship opportunities for the school.

Marcus has a realistic sense of his university's competitiveness for the British scholarships, but he should not sell his school short. He can use publicity from this student's success to develop greater interest in national scholarships.

General Coping Strategies for Dealing with Scholarship Challenges

These six scenarios include suggestions for ways to cope with specific challenges, and the suggestions have several common elements. All rely on one or more of the three basic coping strategies that psychologists identify as forming the backbone to successful stress management. Because each situation presents its own unique features and because each of us has our own particular personality, there is no one best way to cope with stress. Rather than prescribe one type of coping strategy that will always be most successful, we instead recommend that advisors choose the pieces of these three basic strategies that best fit the situation. Each type of strategy has its strengths and weaknesses, however, and advisors should be mindful of that as they seek ways for coping successfully.[1]

PROBLEM-FOCUSED COPING

The stressed person tries to change the actual situation. The first set of solutions provided to these scenarios involves problem-focused coping, such as trying to secure more resources, obtaining comparative data from other institutions, and surveying past students. Advisors are best off using problem-focused coping when a situation actually can be changed. If it is too late to change it or just not possible for any one person to change it, then advisors will need to borrow from another coping strategy.

EMOTION-FOCUSED COPING

The person under stress does not actually change the situation but changes his or her perception of it. In our outlined scenarios, emotion-focused coping includes finding ways to feel better, to evaluate personal biases, and to define success in ways other than winning. Not included but also valuable emotion-focused coping strategies include self-care, which includes taking time, even during heavy deadline season, to exercise, relax, spend time with family, and simply veg out. Emotion-focused coping is best used when an advisor cannot change a situation but needs to have a more positive attitude. Eventually, even though a situation may seem like it cannot be changed, by reducing stress levels the advisor may find changing mental gears creates space to try a new, more successful approach.

SEEKING SOCIAL SUPPORT

Talking to colleagues, particularly other advisors, can help alleviate stress through both problem-focused and emotion-focused coping. Other advisors know better than anyone the many facets of the job and the full range of its highs and lows. They can offer practical advice, helping a stressed advisor feel better by providing a chance to vent. Being the one to give the advice can also be a boost. Giving practical advice may allow some advisors to solve their own problems more effectively, and the shared emotional support will bolster feelings of well-being for everyone concerned. Even brand-new advisors may be able to offer solutions that seasoned advisors have not considered; social support definitely is a mutually rewarding situation.

The job of a fellowships advisor is not without its challenges, but it also carries many benefits. As advisors we have the opportunity to give our students knowledge and skills that can truly change their lives. We can also gain gratification from knowing that we have done the best job we can to help them develop in ways that will benefit not only their fellowship applications but also their prospects for a rewarding and successful career in their graduate years and beyond.

10

Balancing Scholarship and Scholarship Advising

MONIQUE BOURQUE, JANET MYERS, DEBORAH MORGAN OLSEN, AND JOHN ORR

Monique Bourque serves as director of the Office of Student Academic Grants and Awards at Willamette University, where she also teaches environmental history. She has served as the fellowship advisor at Swarthmore College, as an assistant dean in the College of General Studies at the University of Pennsylvania, and as an archivist at several historical libraries in the Philadelphia area. Her primary research interests are social welfare in antebellum America and women nature writers at the turn of the twentieth century.

Janet Myers directs the Office of National and International Fellowships at Elon University, a program she established while serving a four-year term as associate director of the honors program, beginning in 2004. She has since been an active member of NAFA and regularly presents at the national conferences. In addition to her work with fellowship advising, she is an associate professor of English with a specialization in Victorian literature and culture, and she has taught a range of courses at Elon since 2000.

Deborah Morgan Olsen *is the competitive scholarships advisor at Linfield College in McMinnville, Oregon. In addition to working with scholarship applicants, she is an instructor in history. Her areas of research include Richard Champion (an eighteenth-century Quaker from Bristol, England), local history (the music of the Aurora Colony), and women's history (promotional literature of three women's colleges and women's role at the 1905 World's Fair in Portland).*

John Orr *is assistant to the provost for honors and fellowships and grants at the University of Portland. An associate professor of English, he has served as advisor to scholarship applicants since 2006. During that time the University of Portland has ranked among the national leaders in Fulbright Grants for master's-granting universities. When not working on scholarships, he also teaches nineteenth- and early twentieth-century American literature.*

Fellowships advisors come in many forms: the faculty member who advises fellowship applicants; the administrator who teaches in addition to advising duties; the advisor who is also a student, pursuing an advanced degree. Many advisors balance advising and other administrative responsibilities with efforts to maintain an academic identity through teaching, research, and publication because academic work informs and enriches work with students, because such work is crucial to professional success, and because it is personally fulfilling. Balancing roles as an advisor and a faculty member can be challenging. Juggling these responsibilities with intentionality, however, can improve advising, maximize the use of time, and help advisors meet professional academic goals such as publishing and earning promotion and tenure.

This essay examines the challenges involved in reconciling academic accomplishment with administrative duties. It grew out of a panel discussion that included an administrator who taught and maintained an active research and publishing program, an administrator whose primary responsibility was administering academic programs but who advised a steadily increasing stream of fellowship applicants in addition to teaching, and two faculty members who coordinated fellowships in addition to their faculty responsibilities. Shared struggles include negotiating course release time for fellowship advising or time free from administrative duties in order to conduct research and convincing the administration that release time will be spent effectively, making time for class preparation when administrative duties compete for time and application deadlines are pressing, assessing and evaluating shifts in workloads or responsibilities over time, making a case for the importance of fellowship advising within the promotion and tenure process, and finally, doing justice to the remaining competing responsibilities.

We hope this essay will serve as a basis for ongoing discussion of these issues and offer some useful strategies for balancing the competing demands of administration, advising, and academics.

Strategies for Juggling Advising and Teaching

Holding a faculty position that includes teaching courses and administering a fellowship advising program can at times feel schizophrenic, but the challenges associated with this juggling act can be mitigated by treating the two parts of such a position as elements on the same continuum. Such an approach can help advisors recruit more effectively, maximize efficiency, and forge a coherent career. The following three practical strategies can foster this continuum approach.

First, embrace the fluidity of the position. Talk about mentoring students one on one as a form of teaching when speaking with colleagues and administrators, as well as when documenting the work through annual reports and other avenues. Because fellowship advising is a relatively new profession, advisors have the power to influence how this work is perceived and to advocate for the importance of fellowship advising as an alternative form of teaching. For institutions that prioritize teaching, it can be especially important to link advising to the institution's overall mission.

Second, teach an advising course or otherwise engage in group mentoring of national fellowship candidates, whether in person or online. This method is time efficient for advisors juggling roles, since information and advice can be disseminated to small groups of students rather than one on one. Applicants who receive group mentoring may benefit from a shared sense of community, and they can certainly help one another by sharing feedback on essays through peer review or workshop discussion. For those advisors who also teach English, this approach is a natural bridge from teaching writing and puts expertise in that field to good use. It also puts the emphasis of writing application essays on a process of self-discovery rather than on winning or losing a fellowship competition.

Third, advisors can create a continuum by seeking opportunities to work with and teach high-achieving students in contexts outside fellowship advising. Volunteering to teach honors courses or other classes that target unique populations can be very fruitful in enabling advisors to get to know the students they may wish to recruit. Likewise, supporting undergraduate research initiatives on one's campus and mentoring undergraduate research projects also help reinforce the continuity between mentoring/advising and teaching while potentially enhancing the advisor's disciplinary scholarship.

The work of creating a continuum becomes fruitful in the context of an advisor's overall professional development and, particularly, in the tenure and promotion process. Advisors stress to students the importance of creating a coherent narrative to structure their national fellowship essays, and this advice applies to career advancement, as well. Advisors who can show continuity between their teaching and their administrative service through fellowship advising will be able to demonstrate a compelling and coherent career focus, one that includes but is not limited to serving the needs of high-achieving student populations.

Strategies for Juggling Advising, Administration, and Teaching

Faculty members who also have administrative responsibilities inevitably experience moments when teaching is compromised by the immediate demands of the administrative role. When one of those responsibilities is advising students who are applying for major fellowships and grants, at times in the semester teaching understandably becomes a lower priority given the constraints posed by a looming application deadline. Since many advisors entered higher education wanting to interact with students in the classroom, viewing teaching as something that we think about only at the last minute causes some measure of guilt, and faculty members who are also advisors can easily feel as if they are shirking that part of their job. The following suggestions might mitigate that guilt to some extent.

First, faculty/advisors need to remember that once having taught a class a few times, they can reasonably cut back on the amount of preparation devoted to a particular class. Yes, updating is essential, but redesigning the class each time is not. An activity, whether a reading or a specific exercise, that has been used several times may seem a bit stale to the instructor, but it is brand new to the students in the class. Likewise, cutting back on preparation can mean ceding more control of the classroom to the students, thereby allowing them to set more of the agenda and to learn by doing. An organic discussion may emerge when we are less set on making all of the points that we have been preparing for days.

Second, honesty garners understanding. Students need to know that faculty members have other responsibilities that extend beyond teaching their classes and grading their assignments. When a major fellowship or grant is about to go out, explain to the students that the assignments will be returned after that deadline and why that is the case. Just as faculty members need to remember that students have other demands on their time beyond an individual class, they need to recognize the same about faculty. The vast majority of them will.

Finally, advisors must remind themselves that working with students on fellowships and grants is another form of pedagogy and that these two activities are indeed on a continuum. Though you may feel as if teaching occurs only in a classroom, remember that devoting countless hours to drafts of personal statements truly is another kind of pedagogy, one that may in the long run be equally valuable. Time is not always stolen from teaching by advising; it may very well be taken from one type of teaching (what occurs in the classroom) and devoted to another (what occurs in the office).

Strategies for Juggling Advising and Scholarship in a Discipline

Whereas creating a balance between teaching and advising can organically grow out of the similarities between the two roles, finding time for scholarship in a faculty member's discipline is a more challenging task. The key to success here is effectively carving out time for scholarship, which requires both efficient use of time and skill in navigating an institution's political landscape.

Teaching even a less-than-full course load combined with fellowship advising can make academic research and writing impossible during the academic year. Summer can be an excellent time for completing academic work—there are at least no fellowship deadlines in the summer. But faculty who teach in the summer or who have other administrative duties may find that these responsibilities tied with advising work can easily crowd out research during the summer, as well. How can advisors make time for research and writing in the face of such a workload? The two most feasible options may be negotiating a leave or negotiating for contract modifications.

If an institution has no program for allowing paid leave for academic projects, faculty and administrators can often apply for and receive an off-campus assignment that is unpaid, assuming that such an option is affordable. Whether you will be paid for your leave, your chances of being successful in getting it are greatly improved by being well organized before you approach the dean or other administrator who will be responsible for approving your request.

First, before requesting paid or unpaid leave for research, talk with others who have taken such leave at the institution, research the process, and be prepared to create an abstract and/or detailed summary of the project and a timeline. Written support from colleagues in the field or support from other institutions (for example, the archives where the research is going to be conducted) also is helpful. Treating the proposal as though it were a request for grant support (in a way, it is) demonstrates both serious commitment to the endeavor and the significance of the work to the field. For those advisors with an appointment that is primarily administrative, an academic approach reminds the institution that these advisors possess valuable skill sets in addition to administrative and advising expertise. Those who successfully apply for leave should produce work (e.g., a publication or a professional presentation) that will make a future leave more likely. If no work is produced, the higher administration will assume that time away from advising does not produce the intended results.

Another way to secure additional time is to pursue contract changes that will allow more room for academic work or professional activities like conferences. This may involve asking for one or more course releases. Aside from the question of whether the institution can afford to accommodate this request on either a temporary or an ongoing basis, there are two fundamental strategies for improving the odds of being granted a contract adjustment.

First, develop a good track record in scholarship advising, as well as teaching and/or professional activity, before requesting a more favorable contract. Statistics on awardees from the institution may be persuasive, or anecdotal evidence from students may persuade the upper administration of the value of the process.

Second, collect and present data from similar institutions that demonstrate that the current contract is out of line with peer institutions. The nature of the individual advisor's appointment will affect whether providing such information will be persuasive, as will the arrangement of advising at comparable or peer institutions. The effort is worth making, however, and the information can also be useful in justifying other types of support.

Strategies for Creating and Managing Time

If for either practical or political reasons leave or an adjusted contract is not possible, there are still some time-management strategies that may be helpful in creating small spaces of time where academic projects can happen. It may be helpful to consult one of the many books available on completing dissertations, as some of them directly address the issue of managing time in such a way as to maintain project momentum in limited but consistent blocks of time and offer helpful hints on breaking large projects into practical, manageable pieces.[2]

Many institutions and administrators believe that advanced academic training and an ongoing academic program contribute to fellowship advising by making it easier for administrator-advisors to establish and maintain credibility with faculty and by enriching student advising, for both faculty-advisors and administrator-advisors. The pressure of student advising—especially in periods where application levels are increasing—makes teaching more difficult and research and writing virtually impossible, however, at any time except during a leave. Administrators who teach must also walk the line between faculty responsibilities and administrative appointment in such a way as to make clear that they are not hoping to find a back way into a faculty position or gain privileges explicitly reserved for full-time faculty. Teaching administrators must make a careful argument for funding for academic conferences, particularly in current economic conditions, where even attending advisors' conferences may be out of reach.

Regardless of where these small blocks of time for writing or research occur, one of the most difficult challenges will be defending that time in order to move a project forward. There will be moments when approaching deadlines make any endeavors not related to applications simply impossible. At other times the first task will be letting go of guilt over ignoring other forms of academic work. It is vital for advisors to embrace a larger sense of what it means to have an academic identity and to understand that it is in a real sense part of the job. For administrators this acceptance is likely to be particularly difficult, but its importance cannot be overstated. Seeing all aspects of a job as part of an academic endeavor frees advisors to engage in the various aspects of their work with less guilt. Faculty have to be able to focus on scholarship advising without anxiety about teaching or their own academic work, and administrators who are committed to even a modest level of scholarship must block time to work on their projects.

Carving out time for a personal project can be difficult. Answering emails, attending meetings, and meeting with students who really want to get a jump on their fall applications—saying as they sit down that it won't take very long—can make for small distractions, but they quickly add up, eroding a significant amount of time and attention. For academic work as for anything else, getting back up to speed after such interruptions greatly reduces productivity.

Begin by setting aside a small block of time each week for academic work, whether a Monday morning, a Friday afternoon, or even just the lunch hour. Once the time has been established, protect it. Knowing this dedicated time is there waiting each week makes it easier to flex to meet the immediate and urgent challenges of any given day. Not every research afternoon will be incredibly productive, but that time can be used to continue to think about current projects, tinker with a manuscript, or read a relevant article—anything that keeps that part of the brain working on the subject keeps the momentum going and gives the advisor a sense that progress is possible. Giving oneself permission to ignore nonurgent requests during academic work time is extremely difficult but is necessary in order to successfully pursue and complete any academic project.

Setting private goals, in the form of either specific timelines or distinct tasks, can be helpful, whether requesting a leave or contract change or just trying to make effective use of small amounts of time wrested from the work week. Keep goals feasible so that they will be ways to chart progress rather than sources of anxiety. Other ways to create a framework for promoting progress in academic work might include making time to attend an academic conference and if possible present, ideally every year. Regional conferences in some disciplines often are not terribly expensive and can be a solid alternative to more occasional national meetings. Proposing and delivering a paper can provide both an incentive for protecting research time and motivating deadlines for actually producing the work. If presenting at conferences seems to add too much pressure to an already tall and wobbly stack of responsibilities, a writing group can be a helpful but gentler way to encourage or maintain progress on a project, for those who are fortunate enough to have colleagues who can make the time.

The Benefits of These Approaches

For advisors whose primary appointment is administrative rather than academic, fellowship advising can provide a bridge to connect professional activities with scholarship or teaching undertaken in addition to advising responsibilities. Regardless of whether an advisor has a faculty appointment, fellowship advising is a professional activity that cuts across the major areas in which university faculty are required to engage: teaching, research, and service. By juggling intentionally, advisors can capitalize on this complexity and become more effective and more productive in all three areas.

11

Expanding Access through Organized Support
The History and Purpose of the
National Association of Fellowships Advisors

BETH POWERS

Beth Powers is the founder and director of the Office of Special
Scholarship Programs at the University of Illinois–Chicago, where she
has worked since 2000. Previously, she worked in fellowship and prelaw
advising at Kansas State University for four years. For NAFA she has
served as a conference organizer, a member of the ethics committee, a board
member, and vice president. She was president from 2005 to 2007 and is a
founding member.

Before NAFA, you were working by yourself on your campus. Few others understood your joys and challenges; you were alone. It is hugely different now for advisors. NAFA provides a place to learn, to share ideas, to let off steam.

—Jane Curlin, Senior Program Manager,
Udall Foundation Education Programs

Scholarship advising has taken place in one form or another for as long as scholarships have existed. The oldest scholarship, the Rhodes, was created in 1904. The Fulbright was established in 1946; the National Science Foundation Graduate Fellowship, in 1952; and the Marshall Scholarship, in 1953. As more and more Americans began to pursue higher education and postgraduate study in the sixties and the seventies, government and private organizations offered more funding to support students whose achievements matched their interests. The Truman Scholarship was first awarded in 1977–1978; the first Goldwater, in 1986; and the first Udall Scholarship, in 1996. Fellowship advising developed as a profession in response to this growing number of scholarships as universities realized that organizing the competitions and preparing the students took time and effort. The foundations' practice of requesting that university presidents appoint people to recruit students for their awards and shepherd them through the process established the need for a campus facilitator for scholarships. In this way foundations fostered the development of the field of fellowship advising.

By the late 1990s many fellowships advisors and foundation representatives had long realized that supporting students as they applied for nationally competitive awards was valuable as a process in itself, helping to expand those served and increasing student reflection and planning, as well as student success. Nancy Twiss, from Kansas State University, was one of these early scholarship advisors.[1] She played a critical role in the beginning of the National Association of Fellowships Advisors (NAFA), though she retired before the organization was founded. The combination of a growing number of nationally competitive scholarships, the creation of the role of scholarship advisor, and the increasing need for communication between advisors and foundations set the stage for the development of NAFA.[2]

Twiss's work at Kansas State University and that of countless advisors elsewhere demonstrated that universities could indeed provide valuable information and insights to nationally competitive students. Mary Tolar was one such student and won both a Truman and a Rhodes Scholarship during her time as an undergraduate at KSU under the guidance of Nancy Twiss. Tolar went on to play a pivotal role in the founding of NAFA. After graduate study she began working in scholarship advising and eventually, in 1999, took a position with the Truman Foundation with Louis Blair, then its executive secretary. Mr. Blair (as he was called by all applicants and scholars) had long appreciated the role of faculty representatives in the advising process. From the Truman Foundation's perspective, students, universities, and foundations were best served by consistent communication between advisors and foundations.

In 1997 Blair arranged a Truman conference in Roanoke, Virginia, to bring together Truman faculty representatives from around the country. Though the number of institutions that attended was small and only one foundation was present, the event provided a framework and whetted an appetite for subsequent conferences that over time grew into the biennial NAFA conferences, which advisors rely on for scholarship information, support, and professional development.

After Roanoke the Truman Foundation hosted another conference in Valley Forge, Pennsylvania, cohosted by Edwin Goff at Villanova. In 1999 the Truman Foundation partnered with the Marshall Aid Commission for a conference at the University of Arkansas. The university's Suzanne McCray chaired the Fayetteville event, which drew approximately 160 attendees. Nancy Twiss gave the keynote address. The success of this jointly sponsored event and the ever-increasing participation led to discussions between the foundations and the advisors about further collaborations and the inclusion of more foundations.

As Bob Graalman, director of scholar development for Oklahoma State University, states:

I remember the energy of the first meetings, especially the meeting in Fayetteville where Nancy Twiss spoke, and we learned firsthand of the pressures our colleagues were experiencing nationally. The enthusiasm that was on display there was infectious, and I remember thinking that my professional life had changed dramatically just from that event.

In 2000 the Truman Foundation organized two seminal Truman-sponsored conferences, cohosted by the University of Missouri in Columbia and by the University of Massachusetts in Amherst with the help of Richard Hardy and Susan Krauss Whitbourne, respectively. Blair and Tolar spoke to the participants at these events about the need for an advisor-led organization that would facilitate ongoing communication between advisors and foundations.

The Truman Foundation suggested that the growing number of advisors attending the conferences indicated a need for a professional organization. Tolar identified a group of twenty-one advisors who had participated in Truman conferences and contacted them to suggest that they create an organization to provide the kind of support, networking, and foundation relations that advisors seemed to want and need.[3] The group included public and private, large and small, and eastern, midwestern, southern, and western universities. Members of that group met in Chicago in the summer of 2000, where they chose the name the National Association of Fellowships Advisors and created a framework for the organization, setting course for a first conference in the summer of 2001.

At the Chicago meeting, the group also nominated Bob Graalman (Oklahoma State) as its first president, Suzanne McCray (University of Arkansas) as vice president, John Richardson (University of Louisville) as treasurer, and Ann Brown (Ohio University) as secretary. An election was held at the first conference establishing this group as the first executive council for NAFA. The remainder of the group constituted the board. At the first meeting, the board decided to offer biennial conferences alternating with study tours to Europe and regional workshops. The executive group reached out to foundations, soliciting their membership in NAFA, and a subcommittee began work on a constitution and bylaws.

NAFA also sought 501(c)(3) status, which was secured in 2003, and an Oklahoma State University student designed the NAFA logo. The first official NAFA conference was held in Tulsa in the summer of 2001. Bob Graalman led that effort, and the highlight was a dinner at the Gilcrease Museum hosted by the Gates Cambridge Trust, which was inaugurating the Gates Cambridge Scholarship. Nancy Twiss was honored in Tulsa for her contributions to the profession. In 2003 the conference was held in Denver and coordinated by Todd Breyfogle (University of Denver and editor of the *American Oxonian*). NAFA's treasurer, John Richardson, hosted a conference in Louisville with a final banquet at Churchill Downs in 2005. At this meeting, organizers initiated the practice of inviting speakers from outside the scholarship world. Attendees heard from Richard Light, Harvard University professor of education, who spoke about his research for the book *Making the Most of College* as it tied to nationally competitive awards.

In summer 2007 NAFAns traveled to Washington, DC, where Paula Warrick (American University) coordinated events. The British embassy hosted NAFA in a reception at the ambassador's residence, and the group was addressed by U.S. solicitor general Paul Clement, who recounted his experience with scholarships at the Museum of Women and the Arts. To celebrate NAFA's first ten years, the board chose Seattle for its meeting. Mona Pitre-Collins (University of Washington) and Jane Morris (Villanova University) jointly planned the conference. Attendees had the great pleasure of hearing from William Gates Sr. and Anne Udall, sister to Morris and Stewart Udall. The 2011 conference in Chicago was NAFA's largest ever, with over 320 attendees registered. Doug Cutchins (Grinnell College) and Beth Powers served as co-organizers. Addressing the theme of underrepresentation in scholarships, speakers Debbie Bial of the Posse Foundation and John Brown Jr., associate director of the White House Initiative on Historically Black Colleges and Universities, offered valuable perspectives on inclusion and advancement for underrepresented students in the twenty-first century.

As Alicia Hayes, coordinator of the Scholarship Connection at University of California–Berkeley, states:

> Although an increase in membership is usually inevitable, what is remarkable about NAFA's development is how the organization has tried to diversify the membership so that the types of schools are more diverse (e.g., community colleges, HBCUs, and Hispanic serving schools). Also, the organization has sought to highlight concerns and situations by all types of advisors (be they full time, part time, or juggling other duties), all types of institutions (from small liberal arts schools, research schools, large public, small private, or the Ivy League), and has sought to encourage the participation of more members in running NAFA (from participating on committees and hosting workshops to running for the board). I feel that NAFA has developed into a more inclusive organization.

In between the conference summers, NAFA has offered opportunities for members to visit the United Kingdom, Ireland, and Germany, as well as attend regional workshops in the United States. The first trip to the United Kingdom took place in the summer of 2002, where a group visited English and Scottish universities. Ann Brown, Suzanne McCray, and Betsy Vardaman organized the trip. In 2004 Jane Morris, Susan Krauss Whitbourne, Paula Goldsmid (Pomona College), and Mark Bauer (Yale University) coordinated the study tour to England, Scotland, and Ireland. The variety of organizations represented in these leadership efforts indicates the broad support for scholarship applications efforts found across the country in both public and private institutions of varying sizes.

In 2006 NAFA members again traveled to the United Kingdom, but this time, many universities congregated at Cambridge thanks to Gordon Johnson, then provost for the Gates Cambridge Scholarship, thereby reducing in-country travel and giving members a chance to get to know Cambridge better. This group also traveled to Oxford and visited Irish universities. Mary Denyer, assistant secretary and head of the scholarship administration of the Marshall Aid Commission, played a critical role in each of the UK trips, and Dell Prendergast and Mary Lou Hartman (former directors of the Mitchell Scholars Program) provided invaluable assistance with the Irish trips. In 2008 a group visited Germany and the United Kingdom in coordination with Fulbright and the German Academic Exchange Services. Organizers of this trip and the 2011 Germany trip included Lisa Grimes (William and Mary), Amy Eckhardt (Western Kentucky), Ruth Ost (Temple), Laura Damuth (Nebraska–Lincoln), Ken Lavin (Air Force Academy), Cookie Sunkle (Denison), and Denise DellaRossa (Notre Dame). Again, this variety of institutional representation gives an important sense of the increase in schools that value the scholarship application process and that want their advisors to be actively involved in meeting with foundations and more fully understanding what opportunities are available for their students and how students should prepare to compete.

As Elizabeth Vardaman, associate dean for special programs at Baylor University's College of Arts and Sciences, remarks:

> *Membership in NAFA has been wonderful for me professionally and personally. I have gained not only a broad understanding of a vast array of fellowships but also confidence that I can provide valuable resources and*

advice for our student-scholars. In addition, NAFA has offered me the opportunity to participate in the national conversation on issues that matter to my work with scholarships and to the undergirding of liberal education at Baylor.

In 2012 members attended Washington, DC, and UK study tours. Alongside these study tours, two-day regional workshops focused on specific topics have taken place at universities across the country with the leadership of many talented NAFA members. The Washington, DC, tour was the first of its kind, and NAFA members were able to visit the Irish embassy, as well as the British Council's headquarters. Participants also met with NIH, NSF, Goldwater, Truman, Rhodes, Fulbright, Gilman, and Boren scholarship officials.

NAFA has attracted national press attention throughout its history. In an article published in the *Chronicle of Higher Education* in 2001, the question of how much assistance is too much was raised. Foundations and advisors have consistently posed the same question, and NAFA has addressed it head on, with ethics being a focus of every conference and nearly every publication. In addition to developing a constitution and bylaws, which have been amended over time, members approved a code of ethics in 2009. As NAFA has increased in membership, the organization has grown in other formal structures, as well. During her presidency Paula Warrick led the board in generating a strategic plan to see the organization through 2014. Since its beginning in 1999, the NAFA Listserv has provided members with access to valuable input from foundations, advice from colleagues, personal and professional support, and amusing exchanges. The website, initially developed in 2000 by Bill Beesting (Florida International University), includes a link to events and a list of current members, as well as a bulletin board. Members produced a NAFA newsletter in the organization's early years, and past versions are available on the website, including two surveys of the profession that offer valuable, detailed descriptions of the variety of scholarship-advising arrangements on campuses.

As Kyle Mox, senior advisor for scholarships and fellowships at the University of Chicago, affirms:

The most important function of NAFA is its role as the moderator of ethical standards in the sphere of fellowship advising. By establishing codes of ethics for advisors, foundations, and institutions alike, NAFA has established itself as an essential and substantive organization. With the creation of these codes, I as a fellowship advisor have a clear point of reference to guide my own personal decisions, to craft my office operations and policies, and to inform the attitude of my institution in general. NAFA leads by example and it allows me to lead my own students well.

NAFA continues to grow, change, and add to its fundamental mission to "guide advisors in promoting the full potential of fellowship candidates through the application process, and to foster the continued growth and professionalization of fellowship advising in higher education." In finding meaningful ways to support students, the organization and its individual members have often connected with programs designed to help students develop personally, academically, and professionally. Internal scholarships, undergraduate research, service programs, leadership development, and study abroad have grown out of or alongside many scholarship offices, underscoring members' conviction that nationally competitive awards are inextricably linked to helping students find and develop opportunities that allow them to reach their goals. In its relationships with foundations—although the organization tries not to interfere with their work in any way—NAFA closely works with them on common interests, making announcements at conferences and monitoring and sharing opinions on the Listserv and at conferences. As NAFA moves forward into its second decade, it does so with a strong sense of its mission to educate and assist its members, to continue the democratization of the profession, to use technology efficiently and effectively to reach its goals, and most important, to further promote the human connections that nurture members as individuals and as professionals.

12

Performance Review
Reflections on Privilege and Gratitude

JANE MORRIS

Jane Morris is a 1978 graduate of Villanova University with both a BS in biology and a BA in honors. After receiving a master's in biology from Bryn Mawr College, she worked as a research scientist in both the private and public sectors for nearly twenty years. In September 2001 she became Villanova's first director of the Center for Undergraduate Research and Fellowships. In this capacity, she provides guidance for students applying for nationally competitive scholarships and direction for the Presidential Scholarship Program and the Villanova Undergraduate Research Fellowship program. In 2004 and 2006, Jane directed site visits by NAFA members to universities in the United Kingdom, Ireland, and Northern Ireland. She has published two articles on the nationally competitive awards and has served as NAFA's vice president from 2007 to 2009 and its president from 2009 to 2011.

This year, amid meeting scholarship deadlines, tracking down letters of recommendation, and dealing with the politics of departmental budgeting, I am paying especially close attention to the issue of scholarship advising assessment. I have been in this job for more than a decade now, and NAFA has recently made discussion of assessment a priority. As an organization NAFA has a role to play in establishing the standards by which professional practice will be judged. As individuals engaged in the work of helping students discern their academic and professional goals through the lens of nationally competitive scholarships, advisors have a unique set of performance criteria. As one who has witnessed the growth and maturation of this critical role both professionally and personally, I would like to share a few reflections, as well as the profound gratitude I feel for having the privilege to work with the next generation of world leaders.

Like so many of my colleagues, I began with no direct qualifications for the job other than some twenty years doing research and some experience working with college students. My initial supervisor provided a sound foundation for starting an advising program and, even more important, gave me the freedom to explore. NAFA, then in its infancy, also played a critical role by allowing me to take on responsibilities within the organization. One of the best ways to learn something is to be immersed in it (at least, that is what I tell my students), so I learned a great deal about scholarship advising through my leadership roles in NAFA. Similarly, I learned a great deal about university culture and politics by serving on various committees and task forces. Through this service I discovered ways to expand the office to include undergraduate research as a part of its mission, and I also found fruitful partnerships with the honors program, admissions, each of the university's colleges, and the center for multicultural affairs (CMA). Through CMA I found myself participating in the development of our University Diversity Blueprint and began to see that a commitment to expanding access at all levels was at the heart of our enterprise.

In May 2007 I attended the National Conference on Race and Ethnicity in Higher Education (NCORE) in San Francisco, where Villanova's vice president for the CMA invited me to join a contingent of faculty, administrators, and students. I would encourage all advisors to attend this conference. There, at age fifty-one, I discovered I was white. Go figure.

In all that time it never occurred to me the extent to which the choices I had made and the opportunities that had come my way were the result of nothing more than my being born with white skin. This epiphany transformed me in ways I could not have imagined and forever changed the way I do my job.

It all began at the airport on the way to San Francisco. While we were waiting, I had the great fortune to meet the group of eager young students who were on their way to learn the ins and outs of diversity leadership and intergroup dialogue. Among them was a quiet young African American student, Mike, with whom I had a lovely if brief conversation about his major and his plans for the future. He was from North Philadelphia—a particularly challenging section of the city—and he was an English and Spanish double major who planned on taking his education back to his neighborhood as a teacher. As I often do when I meet students, I started talking to him about scholarships—the Fulbright ETA, in particular. He listened politely and said he would consider it. Well, that he did.

At the beginning of the new school year, I received a visit from Mike. He arrived sporting an oversized jacket and a sheepish grin, and he took a seat in my office, slouching down in his chair. He seemed unsure why he was there—but he was there. He told me he had come back from the conference and shared our conversation about the Fulbright with Sr. Rosemary, the nun who ran the afterschool program Mike attended throughout grade school and high school. Sr. Rosemary encouraged Mike to explore the Fulbright and made him promise to come see me. We talked for quite some time about options for ETAs in Spanish-speaking countries, and I could tell that he was still not quite convinced. Even in my post-NCORE awareness, I realized that I needed to pull in some allies to help Mike understand what a strong candidate he was, so I sent him down the hall to meet with my assistant director—someone much closer to his age, fluent in Spanish, and a former Teach for America teacher. Later, I heard from our vice president for multicultural affairs that she too had encouraged Mike to come talk about the Fulbright. I even had a visit from Sr. Rosemary, making sure that Mike had come to see me. We all worked as a team to support his decision to take an academic and cultural risk in applying for—and winning—a Fulbright ETA to Korea.

It was a long process that took Mike on a journey from his home in North Philly to the Philadelphia Main Line to Korea, where he had such an engaging experience that he stayed on and taught English for a second year. Just recently, he and I were once again meeting in my office and talking about his next steps. He told me then that his initial visit was motivated, along with his promise to Sr. Rosemary, by our first conversation at the San Francisco airport. I was stunned—it never occurred to me that a five-minute conversation could have such an impact. Mike is now a first-year law student at Harvard.

As a result of these experiences, I have had to confront how my own perspective as a white, middle-class academic professional colors the way I do business. I need to seize every opportunity to have these five-minute conversations and then to rely on the network of committed and loving individuals that it may take to provide transformative experiences for all students. I am often reminded of the address that William Gates Sr. delivered at our 2009 NAFA conference, in which he talked about the democratizing mission of NAFA:

> When it comes to the hard work of democratizing, you are both a scout and a coach. You find the young people with the most talent, and then you nurture that talent. Perhaps most important of all, you encourage students to believe in themselves. And you also encourage professors to believe in their students.
>
> It is true at all levels there are young people whose potential is much greater than they think it is. Many don't think about fellowship opportunities at all, because they simply aren't encouraged to see their futures in that way. Others assume they're not cut out for the top fellowships. Part of your task is to give them the confidence to be bold when thinking about what's in store for them.

Gates also challenges us to confront outdated, elitist views of what comprises academic and intellectual excellence: "Talent does not manifest itself in just one way." Keeping this in mind, we need to develop new methods for recruiting candidates into the applicant pool for nationally competitive scholarships. For their part, scholarship providers must seek ways to recognize social dimensions of academic excellence: the capacity for building consensus through leadership and a commitment to service within the larger community.

With Gates's words and our university's strategic diversity plan serving as calls to action, I now seek ways to discover scholarship-caliber excellence that do not depend on a standardized, numbers-driven definition.

Our schools are filled with 4.0 students who are extraordinary in many ways but have yet to develop the characteristics of leadership that comprise a Truman or a Marshall scholar. Through our campus discussions of diversity issues, my assistant director and I discovered the work of Dr. William Sedlacek from the University of Maryland. In *Beyond the Big Test: Noncognitive Assessment in Higher Education,* he makes a strong argument for developing tools to measure such qualities. How effectively does a candidate work as a leader in a group setting, deal with adversity, or handle systemic challenges? In our research we discovered that the Gates-Millennium Scholarship program employed characteristics like these to select their scholars. As administrators of Villanova's Presidential Scholarship, we developed an application process including these criteria and changed the award from a tuition-only scholarship to one that included room, board, and books. We also developed a student program for the scholars to encourage a sense of identity and purpose and better build an atmosphere of community among them.

We are now in our fifth year of using noncognitive assessment as a selection tool for the Presidential Scholars. Though we have yet to formally evaluate the success of the program, I can provide anecdotal evidence that we have accomplished what we set out to achieve. Our Presidential Scholars are a diverse group of students who are actively engaged on and off campus, excelling academically, and competing for and winning the Truman, Goldwater, Boren, Fulbright, and Critical Languages scholarships, among others. They are not afraid to take academic risks and are confident enough to ask for help when they need it. They are leaders on campus and have started community organizations such as the Student Run Emergency Housing Unit of Philadelphia (SREHUP), which combats homelessness through outreach and advocacy. They are partners in the annual Presidential Scholarship selection process, managing the interview program as well as the summer orientation for new scholars. Our first class has now graduated, and its members are now attending medical school and law school, teaching English in France, working on Wall Street, serving the poor along the U.S.-Mexico border, and working in an orphanage in Senegal.

Our office has worked hard to refine the concept of academic excellence on our campus. Now, we are faced with developing tools to redefine the notion of success. I recently had a conversation with a university administrator as we prepared for the annual Early Action Candidates' Day, a day when we promote all of our outstanding academic and extra-curricular programs and parade our wonderful students before the newly chosen and their parents. It was a day when a Presidential Scholar alum now working in a Catholic Worker House in Texas was visiting campus to speak about the Catholic Worker Movement. I suggested that she give a presentation to the candidates for the honors program. The adminis-trator hesitated, saying he believed parents were more interested in how much money their children would be earning after college. He acknowl-edged the important work this young woman was doing, but he was not sure parents would understand it as success. Clearly, we have a lot of work to do.

So this leads me back to the idea of assessment. As NAFA begins to explore the tools for assessing the success of scholarship advising, I hope that we can keep in mind the challenge given to us by William Gates Sr. and our mission, as found on the NAFA website, to "to guide advi-sors in promoting the full potential of fellowship candidates through the application process, and to foster the continued growth and profession-alization of fellowship advising in higher education." We have the op-portunity to lead the way in developing inclusive measures for success and for adequately conveying the full import of the work our scholarship candidates are doing in the world. They come to our offices with big ideas about making the world a better place; we help them develop the tools to do this, whether they win scholarships or not. We owe it to them to help others see their successes in meaningful ways.

As I look at my own performance appraisal this year, I am filled with gratitude for the opportunities that I have had to work with such amaz-ing people, to be a part of the changes they are making in the world, and to be a part of an organization such as NAFA that fosters this work and seeks to unlock potential in all students.

Appendix A

NAFA Membership

EXECUTIVE BOARD OF DIRECTORS

Doug Cutchins, President, Grinnell College

Joanne Brzinski, Vice President, Emory University

John Richardson, Treasurer, University of Louisville

Alicia Hayes, Secretary, University of California–Berkeley

Laura Damuth, Board Member, University of Nebraska–Lincoln

David Schug, Board Member, University of Illinois at
    Urbana-Champaign

Susan K. Whitbourne, Board Member, University of Massachusetts
    Amherst

Julia A. Goldberg, Board Member, Lafayette College

Belinda S. Redden, Board Member, University of Rochester

Lyn Fulton, Board Member, Vanderbilt University

Dana Kuchem, Board Member, The Ohio State University

Tony Cashman, Board Member, College of the Holy Cross

Luke Green, Board Member, Seattle University

Kyle Mox, Board Member, University of Chicago

Sue Sharp, Foundation Representative, IIE/Boren

Tara Yglesias, Communications Director, Truman Scholarship Foundation

Nicole Gelfert, Communications Director, University of Central Florida

MEMBER INSTITUTIONS

Albion College
Alma College
American University
Amherst College
Appalachian State University
Arizona State University
Auburn University
Augsburg College
Austin State University
Ball State University
Barnard College
Baruch College, CUNY
Bates College
Baylor University
Benedictine College
Bennington College
Binghamton University
Boise State University
Boston University
Bowdoin College
Brandeis University
Brigham Young University
Brooklyn College
Bryn Mawr College
Butler University
California Institute of Technology
California State Polytechnic
California State University–
    East Bay
Canisius College
Carleton College
Carnegie Mellon University
Carroll University
Carthage College
Case Western Reserve University
Cerritos College

Chapman University
Chatham University
Christopher Newport University
City College of New York, CUNY
Claremont McKenna College
Clemson University
Cleveland State University
Colby College
Colgate University
College of Charleston
College of New Jersey
College of Staten Island
College of the Holy Cross
College of William & Mary
Colorado School of Mines
Colorado State University
Columbia College
Concordia College
Connecticut College
Cornell College
Cornell University
Dartmouth College
Davidson College
Denison University
DePauw University
Dickinson College
Doane College
Drexel University
Duke University
East Tennessee State University
Eastern Carolina University
Eastern Connecticut State
    University
Eastern Illinois University
Eastern Kentucky University
Elizabethtown College

Elmhurst College
Elon University
Emmanuel College
Emory University
Florida International University
Florida State University
Fordham University
Fort Hays State University
Franklin & Marshall College
Furman University
George Mason University
George Washington University
Georgetown University
Georgia Institute of Technology
Georgia Southern University
Georgia State University
Gettysburg College
Grand Valley State University
Grinnell College
Gustavus Adolphus College
Hamilton College
Hampden-Sydney College
Harding University
Harvard College
Hendrix College
Hobart & William Smith Colleges
Hofstra University
Howard University
Illinois State University
Indiana University of PA
Indiana University–Bloomington
Iowa State University
James Madison University
John Brown University
John Jay College of Criminal
    Justice
Johns Hopkins University

Juniata College
Kalamazoo College
Kansas State University
Kean University
Kent State University
Kenyon College
Knox College
Lafayette College
Lehigh University
LeMoyne College
Lenoir-Rhyne University
Lewis & Clark College
Linfield College
Loyola Marymount University
Loyola University Chicago
Loyola University Maryland
Luther College
Lynchburg College
Macalester College
Manhattan College
Marist College
Marshall University
Maryville University
Massachusetts Institute of
    Technology
Mercer University
Mercyhurst College
Miami University of Ohio
Michigan State University
Michigan Technological University
Middlebury College
Middle Tennessee State University
Mississippi State University
Monmouth College
Montana State University
Monterey Institute of Inter. Studies
Montgomery College

Mount Holyoke College
Muhlenberg College
New Mexico State University
New York University
North Carolina Agricultural and
    Technical State University
North Carolina State University
Northeastern University
Northern Arizona University
Northwestern University
Oberlin College
Occidental College
Ohio Northern University
The Ohio State University
Ohio University
Oklahoma State University
Olin College of Engineering
Oral Roberts University
Pace University
Pacific Lutheran University
Park University
Pennsylvania State Behrend
Pennsylvania State University
Pepperdine University
Pitzer College
Pomona College
Portland State University
Princeton University
Providence College
Purdue University
Ramapo College
Reed College
Rice University
RIT–AEP
Roanoke College
Rollins College
Roosevelt University

Rosemont College
Rutgers University
Samford University
San Diego State University
San Francisco State University
Seattle University
Skidmore College
Smith College
South Carolina State University
Southern Illinois University
Stanford University
St. Edward's University
Stevens Institute of Technology
St. John's College–Annapolis
St. John's College–Santa Fe
St. John's University/
    College of St. Benedict
St. Olaf College
Stonehill College
Stony Brook University
SUNY Buffalo
SUNY Cortland
SUNY Geneseo
SUNY New Paltz
Susquehanna University
Syracuse University
Temple University
Tennessee Technological University
Texas A&M University
Texas A&M University–Kingsville
Texas Women's University
Towson University
Trinity College
Truman State University
Tufts University
Tulane University
Union College

United States Air Force Academy
United States Coast Guard
    Academy
United States Military Academy
University of Alabama
University of Alabama–
    Birmingham
University of Arizona
University of Arkansas
University of California–Berkeley
University of California–Davis
University of California–Irvine
University of California–Riverside
University of California–
    Santa Barbara
University of California–
    Santa Cruz
University of Central Florida
University of Chicago
University of Cincinnati
University of Colorado–Boulder
University of Colorado–Denver
University of Connecticut
University of Dayton
University of Delaware
University of Florida
University of Georgia
University of Houston
University of Idaho
University of Illinois–Chicago
University of Illinois–Springfield
University of Illinois–
    Urbana-Champaign
University of Iowa
University of Kansas
University of Kentucky
University of Louisville

University of Maryland–
    Baltimore County
University of Maryland–
    College Park
University of Massachusetts–
    Amherst
University of Memphis
University of Miami
University of Minnesota–
    Twin Cities
University of Mississippi
University of Missouri–Columbia
University of Missouri–
    Kansas City
University of Montana
University of Nebraska–Lincoln
University of Nevada–Reno
University of New Hampshire
University of New Mexico
University of North Carolina–
    Chapel Hill
University of North Carolina–
    Greensboro
University of North Dakota
University of Northern Iowa
University of North Florida
University of North Texas
University of Notre Dame
University of Oklahoma
University of Pittsburgh
University of Portland
University of Puget Sound
University of Reading
University of Rhode Island
University of Richmond
University of Rochester
University of Scranton

University of South Alabama
University of South Carolina
University of South Dakota
University of Southern California
University of Southern Mississippi
University of South Florida
University of Tennessee
University of Texas–Arlington
University of Texas–Austin
University of Texas–Dallas
University of the Pacific
University of Tulsa
University of Vermont
University of Virginia
University of Washington
University of Wisconsin–
    Eau Claire
University of Wisconsin–Madison
Ursinus College
Utah State University
Vanderbilt University
Vassar College
Villanova University
Virginia Commonwealth
    University

Virginia State University
Virginia Tech University
Wake Forest University
Washington and Jefferson
    University
Washington and Lee University
Washington College
Washington State University
Washington University in St. Louis
Wellesley College
Western Carolina University
Western Kentucky University
Western Washington University
Westminster College
West Texas A&M University
West Virginia University
Wheaton College (MA)
Whitman College
Whittier College
Willamette University
Williams College
Worcester Polytechnic Institute
Wright State University
Yale University

Appendix B

NAFA Code of Ethics

Introduction

The National Association of Fellowships Advisors (NAFA) is a professional organization comprised of individuals engaged in the practice of advising college and university students who apply for competitive scholarships and fellowships; institutions of higher education that promote and celebrate the process of applying for competitive scholarships and fellowships as an educational enterprise; and foundations and organizations that administer competitive scholarship and fellowship programs.

The individuals and institutions that participate in and administer competitive scholarships and fellowships have responsibilities and ethical obligations to their students, university communities, foundations, sponsors, funding agencies, and to society as a whole. Inevitably, misunderstandings and conflicts of interest will arise. The membership of NAFA believes that in order to minimize misunderstandings and conflicts as well as make the experience of applying for scholarships more valuable for students' development, advisors, institutions, and students should value the process above the result. The principles and guidelines stated in the following code of ethics are aspirational, providing a framework for participating in and administering competitive scholarship and fellowship programs.

Mission

The mission of the National Association of Fellowships Advisors (NAFA) is to promote the full potential of fellowship candidates through the application process and to foster the continued growth and professional-ization of fellowship advising in higher education.

Vision

The National Association of Fellowships Advisors (NAFA) envisions the highest-quality fellowship advising for every applicant.

Core Values

Integrity. We agree to conduct ourselves responsibly and ethically in our relationships with students, colleagues at our institutions, and each other. We will approach all candidates and scholarships with the goal to maintain integrity in both our relationships and our approach to the scholarship process.

Collaboration. The effectiveness of all individual members and organizations is enhanced when we work together to promote our programs and protect our candidates' best interests.

Respect. The profession and practice of advising for and administering competitive scholarships and fellowships is based on mutual respect and trust for each other and our candidates.

Fairness. We have an obligation to treat candidates and each other fairly, equitably, and in a nondiscriminatory manner.

Expectations of Advisors

Every candidate who prepares an application for a nationally competitive fellowship will be mentored and evaluated in accordance with the stated criteria of the fellowship.

Fellowship advisors will

- balance the wants, needs, and requirements of applicants, fellowship foundations, and home institutions; advisors' overriding concern must be for student well-being, the integrity of their home academic institution, and the value of the process of applying for fellowships;

- encourage the intellectual autonomy and passion of character of each student with whom they interact;
- encourage students to self-assess their qualifications for individual fellowships and to be realistic in their expectations of the process and the outcome;
- support a campus culture around fellowships that emphasizes consistent and fair promotion of fellowships, as well as awareness of the connections between campus strengths and specific fellowships;
- understand and effectively represent the specific selection criteria and goals of each fellowship as described in foundation materials and convey them with fidelity to candidates;
- announce and promote scholarship and fellowship opportunities broadly, with adherence to the foundations' stated criteria;
- educate the home institution's administration and faculty about fellowship opportunities and ethical practices, including the campus role in student preparation and realistic expectations for fellowship results;
- respect foundation practices and maintain professionalism in all correspondence;
- avoid the appearance or an actual conflict of interest;
- ensure fairness and nonbias in interactions with candidates in fellowship processes;
- not accept gifts from students, faculty, foundations, or administrators where there might be the appearance of a conflict of interest;
- insist upon applicants' adherence to the highest ethical standards in preparing and submitting applications and supporting materials.

Advisor Expectations of Applicants

Prior to applications candidates will

- engage in self-reflection, assess long-term goals, and search for appropriate programs and funding;
- pursue fellowships that support those goals, not fellowships that they must bend their goals to fit;
- be aware of the high level of competition and respect the value of the process.

During the applications process, candidates should

- ensure that all application materials, including but not limited to personal statements, résumés, proposals, and essays, are the sole and original work of the applicant and cite any sources quoted or paraphrased;
- respond to campus and foundation communications in an honest and timely fashion;
- apply only to those fellowships in which they have a genuine interest;
- provide adequate and accurate information to recommenders in a timely fashion;
- neither compose their own letters for faculty to sign, even at the request of faculty, nor ask faculty members to show them their own letters of recommendation;
- make clear what information revealed to an advisor or recommender should remain confidential;
- include résumé and application response items that reflect an accurate and substantive contribution;
- provide honest responses to questions in all practice and real interviews without aggrandizing accomplishments or providing deliberately misleading information to committee members;
- treat other applicants with respect and courtesy.

Guidelines for Institutions

Colleges and universities with students participating in or likely to participate in competitions for major fellowships bear certain ethical responsibilities both to the students and to the foundations and programs.

Those institutions will

- support procedures whose aims are to provide a means of distinguishing merit among applicants for nomination or rating;
- supply accurate and thorough letters of endorsement and actively encourage writers of letters of recommendation to do the same;
- understand fellowship nomination criteria and advise and nominate students appropriately;

- maintain records of the institution's participation in major fellow-ship competitions and protect those records in accordance with federal guidelines;
- emphasize, through publicity and infrastructure, the value of students' intellectual and personal development through the fellowship process;
- when evaluating scholarship programs, use techniques that attempt to measure the value of the process of applying for fellowships and take into account the highly competitive nature of fellowship competitions.

Guidelines for Foundations

Foundations and organizations that administer scholarship and fellow-ship programs have certain ethical responsibilities and obligations to applicants, faculty representatives, university administrators, institutions, and their funding agencies.

Foundations should

- accurately represent the goals, mission, and requirements of the fellowship and of the foundations;
- convey information on eligibility, selection criteria, and application processes in a clear and timely manner;
- select scholars and fellows based on previously published selection criteria, selection procedures, and program goals;
- conduct fair and transparent selection processes, evaluating applicants on the basis of individual qualifications;
- respond quickly, courteously, and professionally to inquiries from faculty representatives and potential applicants;
- respond to advisor feedback as time and relevant policy and law allows;
- refrain from involvement in personal relationships with students, faculty representatives, or other university personnel when such relationships might result in either the appearance of or an actual conflict of interest;
- not accept gifts from students, faculty, or administrators where there might be an appearance of a conflict of interest;

- observe all relevant foundation policies and national and international laws as they relate to the scholarship process;
- endeavor to maintain the faculty representative as the primary point of contact in all matters relating to the award.

Adopted July 2009 by vote of the membership.

Notes

Chapter Three: Enough about Me, What Do You Think about Me?

1. Throughout this essay the term *panelist* describes a member of a Truman Regional Review Panel. The Regional Review Panels meet at locations throughout the country to interview finalists and select Truman Scholars. *Reader* describes a member of the Truman Finalist Selection Committee. The Finalist Selection Committee meets prior to the Regional Review Panels and selects finalists based on the written application.

2. See "Practice Questions for Truman Interviews," Truman Foundation website, http://truman.gov//for-faculty-reps/from-the-foundation/practice-questions-for-truman-interviews.

3. See "2012–2013 Bulletin of Information," Truman Foundation website, http://truman.gov//for-faculty-reps/2013-competition/2013-bulletin-of-information.

4. A question we often receive is whether this portion of the day counts as part of the interview process. This session is so short and the interactions so perfunctory that it would be nearly impossible for a finalist to make a lasting impression—either positive or negative. Finalists should not worry about this portion of the day. If they meet the panelists, fine. If not, they will have ample time during the interview.

5. Again, this is not fatal. One recent Truman Scholar closed his interview with a screed against the Truman process on his campus. According to him, several wonderful Truman candidates were turned away because his campus relied too heavily on GPAs. Several panelists were upset that he used this forum to air his grievances, but they voted to select him anyway.

6. See "Regional Review Panels," Truman Foundation website, http://www.truman.gov/for-candidates/regional-review-panels.

Chapter Five: Preparing Students to Apply for Competitive Law Schools

1. There are no good statistics regarding lawyer satisfaction. Law schools do not, in general, bother to survey their graduates in this regard. I base my comment on the following: (1) personal experiences with law school classmates,

clients' parents (often lawyers), and clients (who years after I helped them go to law school, report back to me regarding how they are faring); (2) frequent discussions of this matter with the career services directors at various law schools, nearly all of whom report that a distressingly large percentage of graduates seem somewhat or very unhappy in their professional lives; (3) the substantial literature that has developed; early examples include Deborah L. Arron, *Running from the Law: Why Good Lawyers Are Getting Out of the Profession* (Berkeley, CA: Ten Speed Press, 1991); Deborah L. Arron, *What Can You Do with a Law Degree? A Lawyer's Guide to Career Alternatives Inside, Outside, and Around the Law* (Seattle: Niche Press, 1992); and Hindi Greenberg, *The Lawyer's Career Change Handbook: More Than 300 Things You Can Do with a Law Degree* (New York: Avon Books, 1998); and (4) the cottage industry devoted to helping lawyers bear the stress and dissatisfaction they feel. This field too has its consultants and substantial literature. Early examples include Walt Bachman, *Law v. Life: What Lawyers Are Afraid to Say about the Legal Profession* (Rhinebeck, NY: Four Directions Press, 1995); Julie M. Tamminen, *Living with the Law: Strategies to Avoid Burnout and Create Balance* (Chicago: ABA Section of Law Practice Management, 1997); and Richard W. Moll, *The Lure of the Law: Why People Become Lawyers and What the Profession Does to Them* (New York: Penguin Books, 1990).

2. In my book *How to Get into the Top MBA Programs,* 6th ed. (New York: Prentice Hall, 2012), I note the views of the admissions directors of leading business schools on different types of applicants. In a chart, I catalog those views from which a typical lawyer applicant is likely to suffer: (1) lacks quantitative abilities, (2) unable to work with others, (3) unlikely to adopt business perspective, (4) arrogant, (5) whiner, and (6) running away from law, not toward business. MBA programs do accept some—but not many—lawyers but perform a rigorous analysis to make sure that the ones they accept do not suffer from these disabilities.

3. Susan Dalessandro, Lisa Stilwell, Jennifer Lawlor, and Lynda Reese, "LSAT Performance with Regional, Gender, and Racial/Ethnic Breakdowns: 2003–2004 through 2009–2010 Testing Years," *LSAT Technical Report Series* 10, no. 3, (2010): 19.

4. Although most admissions directors know that the best estimate of applicants' abilities, as measured by an exam such as the LSAT, is the average of their scores rather than one or the other, they may be swayed from using the average or only the average by two factors. First, they know many people take the test once just to see whether they can score well enough to warrant applying to law school. They often do so without much preparation. As a result, they tend to score substantially below their potential. The same is true for those who feel that their lives depend upon their score and are therefore so nervous they botch the exam. In both cases admissions directors might feel that a later test result could give a more accurate picture of these applicants' abilities. The more jaundiced but no less important second factor is that the all-important *U.S. News & World Report* rankings of law schools substantially depend upon the schools' LSAT

numbers—specifically, the twenty-fifth percentile and seventy-fifth percentile scores of incoming first-year students. This reality gives schools an incentive to admit those with at least one relatively high LSAT score. For instance, consider a law school faced with a choice between two students it deems of identical value apart from their LSAT results. The first took the test just once, scoring a 165; the second took it twice, scoring 162 and 168. Although a school might judge the LSAT results to be equal—assuming it averaged the second candidate's scores and considered that he or she thus had a 165—it would presumably still prefer the second candidate because the score it would report to *U.S. News* would be the 168 not the 165 average, and the 168 would tend to have a more favorable impact upon the school's ranking. (If the school believed that the second candidate's second, higher score was a more accurate indication of her ability, it would presumably accept her on that basis. For instance, she might be a foreign applicant who had never before encountered an American-style standardized exam, strongly suggesting that her first effort should not be given the same weight as the second.)

5. See "2013 Application," Duke Law website, http://law.duke.edu/admis/degreeprograms/jd/#howtoapply.

Chapter Six: Welcoming African Americans to the World of International Scholarships

1. Raisa Belyanvina and Rajika Bhandari, "Increasing Diversity in International Careers: Economic Challenges and Solutions," *Partners Soar,* IIE website, November 2011, http://www.iie.org/Research-and-Publications/Publications-and-Reports/IIE-Bookstore/Increasing-Diversity-International-Education.

2. See also Starlett Craig, "Top 10 Reasons for African American Students to Study Abroad," *Transitions Abroad,* July/August 1998, http://www.transitionsabroad.com/listings/study/articles/studyjul1.shtml; University of Pittsburgh Study Abroad Office, *The World Is in Your Hands Student Guide: African Americans Speak Out and Share Their International Experiences* (Pittsburgh: University of Pittsburgh, n.d.), http://www.ucis.pitt.edu/aie/resources/TWIIYH.pdf; "Boren Scholarships and Fellowships," Diversity Abroad website, http://www.diversityabroad.com/partner/boren-scholarships-and-fellowships/scholarship/Boren%20Fellowship-1631; Peter Schmidt, "Race Plays Key Role in Decision to Study Abroad or to Stay Home, Study Finds," *Chronicle of Higher Education,* September 20, 2010, http://chronicle.com/article/Race-Plays-Key-Role-in/124549/?sid=at&utm_source=at&utm_medium=en; Mark Salisbury, "We're Muddying the Message on Study Abroad," *Chronicle of Higher Education,* July 30, 2012, http://chronicle.com/article/Were-Muddying-the-Message-on/133211; Jinous Kasravi, "Moving beyond the Barriers: Factors Influencing the Decision to Study Abroad for Students of Color" (presentation, CIEE 2009 Annual Conference, Istanbul, Turkey, November 14, 2009), CIEE website, http://www.ciee.org/conference/downloads/past/istanbul/JinousKasravi.pdf.

Chapter Seven: Honoring the Code

1. For a summary of extensive research on the efficacy of honor codes, see Donald McCabe, Linda Trevino, and Kenneth Butterfield, "Cheating in Academic Institutions: A Decade of Research," *Ethics and Behavior* 11 (3): 219–32. See also Miguel Roig and Amanda Marks, "Attitudes toward Cheating before and after the Implementation of a Modified Honor Code: A Case Study," *Ethics and Behavior* 16 (2): 163–71.

2. According to Donald McCabe and Patrick Drinan, "Toward a Culture of Academic Integrity," *Chronicle of Higher Education,* October 15, 1999, http://chronicle.com/article/Toward-a-Culture-of-Academic/15639, "Few programs promote academic integrity among all segments of the campus community. Most institutions do little more than inform their students that a policy on academic integrity exists, sometimes accompanied by a brief discussion of its major points. Many don't draw attention at all to their policies, or fail to advise their part-time faculty members about them."

3. National awards offices are an excellent place to help promote academic integrity policies to both students and faculty. Many offices have a good understanding of these policies and implement them in their daily work.

4. Two-thirds is the number most often cited from McCabe's studies. According to Angela Miller, Tamera Murdock, Eric Anderman, and Amy Poindexter, "Who Are All These Cheaters? Characteristics of Academically Dishonest Students," in *Psychology of Academic Cheating,* edited by Eric Anderman and Tamera Murdock (Burlington, MA: Elsevier Academic Press, 2006), 10, the number can range from "5–95 across 46 studies of cheating. The variation in these numbers is most likely due to carried definition of cheating as well as to measurement methods."

5. Richard Pena-Perez, "Studies Find More Students Cheating, with High Achievers No Exceptions," *New York Times,* September 7, 2012, http://www.nytimes.com/2012/09/08/education/studies-show-more-students-cheat-even-high-achievers.html?_r=0.

6. Julie Zauzmer and Xi Yu, *Conning Harvard: Adam Wheeler, the Con Artist Who Faked His Way into the Ivy League* (Guilford, CT: Lyons Press, 2012), 10–11.

7. Ibid., 113–17.

8. Ibid., 168–71.

9. Zauzmer points out that Adam Wheeler's story on its own is not very important. It is, however, an example of the larger problem of enormous pressure being place upon students from a very young age, a pressure to go beyond being merely successful to being stars who can be admitted to top schools and shine brightly once there. See Zauzmer, *Conning Harvard,* 10–11.

10. See "National Association of Fellowships Advisors Code of Ethics," NAFA website, July 2009, http://www.nafadvisors.org/ethics.php. See also appendix B of this volume.

11. Unfortunately, even plagiarism committed during class is not always consistently addressed at universities across the country. According to Donald McCabe and associates, faculty members are more likely to turn students over to review boards if the institution has an honor code. See Donald McCabe, Kenneth Butterfield, and Linda Trevino, "Faculty and Academic Integrity: The Influence of Current Honor Codes and Past Honor Code Experiences," *Research in Higher Education* 44, no. 3 (June 2003): 368.

12. We began proactively addressing this issue five years ago at the University of Arkansas, and we no longer see student-written letters of recommendation.

13. Faculty members understand the level of vigilance this requires, and when it is not forthcoming from master's level and doctoral level work, the consequences can be severe. See "Ohio U. Panel Rules in Plagiarism Cases of 3 Engineering Students," *Chronicle of Higher Education,* October 23, 2006, http://chronicle.com/article/Ohio-U-Panel-Rules-in/37729. "An investigation sparked by a former graduate student found that plagiarism at the university's Russ College of Engineering and Technology had been 'rampant and flagrant' over the past two decades. The university has already disciplined some faculty members, and it has notified graduates suspected of plagiarism that they must forfeit their degrees, contest the charges, or ask to rewrite their theses." The faculty members who were disciplined were simply not practicing due diligence.

14. Vijaysree Venkatraman, "Convention of Scientific Authorship," *Science,* April 16, 2010, http://sciencecareers.sciencemag.org/career_magazine/previous _issues/articles/2010_04_16/caredit.a1000039.

15. Ibid.

16. Ibid.

17. Ibid.

18. Andrew Brownstein, "Ambitious Colleges End the Ivy Lock on Prestigious Fellowships," *Chronicle of Higher Education,* September 14, 2001, http://chronicle.com/article/Ambitious-Colleges-End-the-Ivy/11018.

19. Louis Blair, "Having a Winner Every Time in the Truman Scholarship," in *Beyond Winning: National Scholarship Competitions and the Student Experience,* edited by Suzanne McCray (Fayetteville: University of Arkansas Press, 2005), 33–49.

20. Eliot Gerson, "Rhodes Scholarship Address" (NAFA Conference, Chicago, June 22, 2011). For videos of the address, go to http://www.youtube.com/channel/UCPmuOabjXSm8BcO5-KPNWvw.

21. Ed Dante, "The Shadow Scholar: The Man Who Writes Your Students' Papers Tells His Story," review of *The Shadow Scholar: How I Made a Living Helping College Kids Cheat,* by Dave Tomar, *Chronicle of Higher Education,* November 12, 2010, http://chronicle.com/article/The-Shadow-Scholar/125329.

22. Richard Light, *Making the Most of College: Students Speak Their Minds* (Cambridge: Harvard University Press, 2001), 10.

23. Immanuel Kant, "The Theory of Ethics," translated by T. K. Abbott, in

Kant Selections, edited by Theodore Meyer Greene (New York: Scribner's Sons, 1957), 309.

24. "National Association of Fellowships Advisors Code of Ethics," NAFA website, July 2009, http://www.nafadvisors.org/ethics.php.

Chapter Eight: Recalculating

1. Andrew Delbanco, "College at Risk," *Chronicle of Higher Education,* February 26, 2012, http://chronicle.com/article/College-at-Risk/130893. This story is also told in Delbanco's new book *College: What It Was, Is, and Should Be* (Princeton, NJ: Princeton University Press, 2012), 15–16.

2. Lincoln Steffens, *A Boy on Horseback/Seeing New York First,* vol. 1 of *The Autobiography of Lincoln Steffens* (New York: Harcourt Brace, 1931), 119.

3. Richard J. Light, *Making the Most of College: Students Speak Their Minds* (Boston: Harvard University Press, 2001), 88.

4. Ibid., 90–91.

5. Mark Edmundson, "Education's Hungry Hearts," *New York Times,* March 31, 2012, http://www.nytimes.com/2012/04/01/opinion/sunday/educations-hungry-hearts.html.

6. Delbanco, *College,* 177.

7. Mark Lilla as quoted in Delbanco, *College,* 14.

8. William Deresiewicz, "Solitude and Leadership: If You Want Others to Follow, Learn to Be Alone with Your Thoughts," *American Scholar,* Spring 2010, http://theamericanscholar.org/solitude-and-leadership.

9. David Brooks, "It's Not about You," *New York Times,* May 30, 2011, http://www.nytimes.com/2011/05/31/opinion/31brooks.html.

10. Carol Geary Schneider, "'Degrees for What Jobs?' Wrong Question, Wrong Answers," *Chronicle of Higher Education,* May 1, 2011, http://chronicle.com/article/Degrees-for-What-Jobs-Wrong/127328.

11. Derek Bok as quoted in Delbanco, *College,* 149.

12. Deresiewicz, "Solitude and Leadership."

13. Delbanco, *College,* 29.

14. John Alexander Smith as quoted in Delbanco, *College.*

15. The phrase "talking rot" is memorably and colorfully expounded upon in Delbanco, *College,* 29.

16. Jeremy Haefner and Deborah L. Ford, "The Double Helix: A Purposeful Pathway to an Intentional and Transformational Liberal Education," *Liberal Education* 96 (2): 50–55.

17. The leaders of this session asked NAFAns to list outcomes that students realize from applying for fellowships. They consolidated the information provided by the participants. The results are reprinted in Figure 2 with permission from Schaarschmidt, Fiori, and Dailinger.

18. For the executive summary and the LEAP initiative, see National Leader-

ship Council for Liberal Education and America's Promise, *College Learning for the New Global Century: Executive Summary with Employers' Views on Learning Outcomes and Assessment Approaches* (Washington, DC: Association of American Colleges and Universities, 2008), https://www.aacu.org/leap/documents/GlobalCentury_ExecSum_3.pdf.

19. Richard Arum and Josipa Roksa, *Academically Adrift: Limited Learning on College Campuses* (Chicago: University of Chicago Press, 2011). This quotation is from Arum and Roksa's "Academically Adrift: Limited Learning on College Campuses" (presentation, AAC&U Annual Meeting, San Francisco, January 28, 2011), https://www.aacu.org/meetings/annualmeeting/AM11/documents/AcademicallyAdriftAACUJan2011.pdf.

20. Alice Stone Ilchman, Warren F. Ilchman, and Mary Hale Tolar, eds., *The Lucky Few and the Worthy Many: Scholarship Competitions and the World's Future Leaders* (Bloomington: Indiana University Press, 2004). This quotation is paraphrased from points made by these editors at a NAFA conference.

21. Delbanco, *College,* 54. He continues a few paragraphs later to reemphasize this point, writing, "It is hard to overestimate the importance of this idea of lateral learning."

22. Deresiewicz, "Solitude and Leadership." He adds, "The best writers write much more slowly than everyone else, and the better they are, the slower they write."

23. John McPhee, "The Writing Life: Editors and Publishers," *New Yorker,* July 2, 2012, 37. McPhee adds, "As a writing teacher, I have repeated that statement to two generations of students. If they are writers, they will never forget it."

24. Drew Gilpin Faust, "By the Book," *New York Times Book Review,* May 24, 2012, http://www.nytimes.com/2012/05/27/books/review/drew-gilpin-faust-by-the-book.html.

25. Seamus Heaney, "Postscript," in *Opened Ground: Selected Poems, 1966–1996* (New York: Farrar, Straus and Giroux, 1998), 411.

Chapter Nine: Coping with Common Challenges

1. For more information, see "Stress Management: How to Reduce, Prevent, and Cope with Stress," *Helpguide.org,* http://www.helpguide.org/mental/stress_management_relief_coping.htm; Mayo Clinic Staff, "Tips for Coping with Stress at Work," Mayo Clinic website, June 26, 2010, http://www.mayoclinic.com/health/coping-with-stress/SR00030; "Stress in the Workplace," APA website, http://www.apa.org/helpcenter/workplace-stress.aspx; and Susan Krauss Whitbourne, "Fulfillment at Any Age: How to Remain Productive and Healthy into Your Later Years," *Psychology Today* website, October 5, 2010, http://www.psychologytoday.com/blog/fulfillment-any-age/201010/the-sweet-smell-failure.

2. For example, see Joan Bolker, *Writing Your Dissertation in Fifteen Minutes a Day: A Guide to Starting, Revising, and Finishing Your Doctoral Thesis* (New

York: Owl Books, 1998); David Sternberg, *How to Complete and Survive a Doctoral Dissertation* (New York: St. Martin's Griffin, 1981).

Chapter Eleven: Expanding Access through Organized Support

1. Nancy Twiss worked at Kansas State University from 1967 to 1995. Her dedicated scholarship advising efforts were ultimately recognized by her promotion to special assistant to the provost for scholarships. According to current KSU advisor Jim Hohenbary, "She introduced to the campus that the scholarship process could be inherently valuable to students." She built a tradition of national scholarship success at KSU that included eight Rhodes, eight Marshall, nineteen Truman, and twenty-three Goldwater scholars during her tenure. She served as mentor and advisor to several of NAFA's founding members. In retirement she divides her time between Kansas, Minnesota, and Canada.

2. This reflection on NAFA's origins owes a deep debt to many NAFA founders, officers, and members whose memories of the organization's development inform this history. I would like to thank Jane Curlin, Bob Graalman, Suzanne McCray, Jane Morris, John Richardson, Jay Shivamoggi, Mary Tolar, Betsy Vardaman, and Paula Warrick for their valuable input to this recounting of NAFA's history.

3. The 2000 NAFA Founding Board Members and their institutions are Bill Beesting, Florida International University; Mary Borg, University of North Florida; Ann Brown, Ohio University; Tamara Cissna, University of Tulsa; Lori Colliander, University of Washington; Jane Curlin, Willamette University; James Duban, University of North Texas; Scott Furtwengler, Southern Illinois University; Edwin Goff, Villanova University; Bob Graalman, Oklahoma State University; Anthony Lisska, Denison College; Norah Martin, University of Portland; Suzanne McCray, University of Arkansas; Beth Powers, University of Illinois–Chicago; Gale Rhodes, University of Louisville; John Richardson, University of Louisville; Lia Rushton, University of Alabama–Birmingham; Mary Tolar, Truman Foundation; Elizabeth Vardaman, Baylor University; Sylvia Whitman, Rollins College; and Michael Young, Arizona State University.

Index